THE Elizabeth:

PASSAGE OF A QUEEN

THE Elizabeth:

Drawings by Martin Pickwick

PASSAGE OF A QUEEN

by Leonard A. Stevens

New York  *Alfred·A·Knopf* *1968*

THIS IS A BORZOI BOOK
PUBLISHED BY ALFRED A. KNOPF, INC.

First Edition
Copyright © 1968 by Leonard A. Stevens
All rights reserved under International and
Pan-American Copyright Conventions.
Published in the United States by
Alfred A. Knopf, Inc., New York, and
simultaneously in Canada by Random
House of Canada Limited, Toronto.
Distributed by Random House, Inc., New York.
Library of Congress Catalog Card Number: 68-23958
The poem "Bon Voyage" by Sir Alan Herbert
is reprinted with the permission of the author.
Manufactured in the United States of America

To my son Timothy

Foreword

When I first heard the news that both of the great *Queen* liners were to be retired before the end of 1968 it came as a deep personal shock because during the thirty years that have passed since I joined the *Queen Mary* as a Junior Navigating Officer early in 1938, these two remarkable ships, somehow, have woven themselves into the tapestry of my life, and I am very proud to have flown my flag as Commodore in *Queen Elizabeth* since January 1966.

Queen Mary with thirty-one years' and *Queen Elizabeth* with twenty-eight years' service have had eventful lives, during which many like myself have developed a real affection for them. We have watched *Queen Mary* capture the Blue Riband in those far-off prewar days; marveled at their splendid wartime record, when each ship was bringing the equivalent of a division of troops at a time, unescorted, across the Atlantic; seen them in those years of great prosperity after the war, sailing voyage after voyage booked to capacity . . . one wonders if there can ever be anything to quite compare with these two wonderful ships. Surely the same thing must be said of them as was said of Sir Winston Churchill—"We shall never see their like again"—and their passing must mark the end of an era and the beginning of a new one.

Leonard Stevens has, in this carefully observed and meticulously detailed account of an ocean crossing in the *Queen Elizabeth,* captured much of the atmosphere that will enable a great lady to live on in our hearts long after she has crossed the North Atlantic for the last time.

One of the oldest British traditions is summed up in those famous words, "The Queen is dead, long live the Queen!" The Cunard Line's many friends will be glad to know that during her last year of service, the cream of the Line's sea staff will be col-

lected on board the *Queen Elizabeth* to form the finest team available to transfer in December 1968 to take the *Queen Elizabeth 2*
away on her maiden voyage.

G. T. Marr, D.S.C., R.O.
Commodore

R.M.S. *Queen Elizabeth*
Southampton
November 14, 1967

Acknowledgments

Most of the sources for this book were found on the R.M.S. *Queen Elizabeth* during and after her 424th commercial voyage. Commodore Geoffrey T. Marr, who headed up the Cunard Line fleet and was Captain of the *Elizabeth,* made it possible for me to reach the sources as the ship proceeded on Voyage 424. The result was nearly thirty hours of tape recorded interviews with dozens of crew members and officers. The Commodore also gave me the opportunity to see all parts of the huge steamship while she was in operation. On my return trip from Europe aboard the *Elizabeth* and on a dozen or more subsequent stopovers in New York the Commodore and his staff continued helping me gather material. Many times at Manhattan's Pier 92 Commodore Marr allowed me to come to his quarters for his help. He patiently answered question after question, even concerning minute details. Later he read the manuscript twice to ensure the accuracy of the work. For all their cordial and cooperative efforts in behalf of this book I wish to thank all the officers and crew of the *Queen Elizabeth*. I direct a particularly large measure of thanks to Commodore Marr.

Behind this opportunity to work aboard the ship were the efforts made by the New York public relations staff of the Cunard Steam-Ship Company Ltd. The Manager of the department, George L. O'Reilly, liked the idea of doing a firsthand account of the *Elizabeth,* and he took charge of all the official arrangements necessary. Then he and his staff, Robert Golrick, Edward Livingston, James Murray, and their secretaries, continually and patiently provided assistance in gathering material for the book and in finally checking its accuracy. A fifth member of the staff, George Bigelow, spent a lot of time and effort to help me gather the illustrative material for the book. In Southampton my finding material and illustrations was guided by a Cunard information officer, John Smith. To all of these people, and to the Cunard Line, I extend my deepest appreciation and thanks.

Several people not at all connected with Cunard gave of their knowledge to make this a better piece of work. I want to mention two in particular:

Frank Braynard of the Moran Towing and Transportation Company in New York is considered one of the nation's leading authorities on passenger steamships. Frank graciously lent me material and illustrations from his impressive collection. He also read the manuscript for the sake of accuracy. If somewhere in this book the *Queen Elizabeth* is referred to as "it" rather than "she," the fault is mine and not that Frank didn't try.

A few years ago Captain Robert Rennie retired from a career as a pilot on the Panama Canal and settled in a house up the road from mine in New Milford, Connecticut. He knows too much about ships for me not to have asked him to read this manuscript in behalf of saving a neighbor from errors in nautical terminology. He tried very hard.

To both Frank and Captain Rennie, my thanks.

Leonard A. Stevens

New Milford, Connecticut
November 30, 1967

Contents

Illustrations

Plates

Following page 142

(Unless otherwise credited, photographs are by the author.)

The Sandy Hook pilot boards the *Queen Elizabeth*

As seen from the main deck, the *Queen Elizabeth* steams under the Verrazano-Narrows Bridge

Map

THE Elizabeth:

PASSAGE OF A QUEEN

Chapter I

Voyage 423: Into New York Harbor

At 7:30 that morning of April 12, the U.S. Coast Guard cutter *Manitou* left the Battery at the tip of New York's Manhattan Island. She sailed south-southwest by Governors Island (on the port side) and the Statue of Liberty (on the starboard side), and in a few minutes her Captain, Charles R. Finn, was heading for the Narrows, the deep mouth of water between Brooklyn and Staten Island.

It was a brilliantly clear morning, and the great harbor was spotted with snubby little tugboats, small workaday lighters, large ferries, colorful cargo ships, and all the other vessels found in the nation's busiest port. Ahead of the *Manitou,* the magnificent Verrazano-Narrows Bridge contrasted with the blue morning sky. The atmosphere, ordinarily dirtied by smog, was so unusually clear that several of the cutter's passengers stood at the outside rails to admire the scenery.

They were a varied group of men, including uniformed officials of the U.S. Customs Bureau, Public Health Service, and Immigration Service; reporters and photographers representing newspapers in New York, Canada, and Great Britain; and three officials of the Cunard Steam-Ship Company Limited. All were on their way to assignments aboard the largest ocean liner in the world, the British Royal Mail Ship *Queen Elizabeth,* scheduled to dock at 11 a.m. The ship, owned by Cunard, was entering the harbor after a short cruise from New York to Bermuda.

Soon after the *Manitou* passed under the heavily trafficked Verrazano Bridge, she was bearing southeast by Coney Island through the buoys that mark the famous Ambrose Channel, the main water highway between New York Harbor and the open sea. The Channel extends about a dozen nautical miles from the Narrows to the tiny Ambrose Lightship (now replaced by a fixed light). Shortly after passing Long Island's Rockaway Point, the cutter's passengers had their first glimpse of the *Elizabeth* steaming slowly into Ambrose Channel through a thin veil of fog. One at a time, the government officials, the press representatives, and the Cunard officials moved to the cutter's port rails for a look at the huge vessel. She appeared to grow larger and larger—to almost unbelievable proportions—as they approached her starboard quarter.

Captain Finn reduced the *Manitou*'s speed as he paralleled the big ship's black hull, bringing his boat alongside a shell door that had been opened from the inside a few feet above the liner's water line. In the door stood the ship's Day Officer and two seamen, three specks against the high walls of riveted steel rising up out of the sea. The *Manitou* rolled as she crossed the liner's bow wave but as she closed in on the great hull, the going smoothed out, and Captain Finn quickly came alongside the liner's open door.

A line was thrown to the *Elizabeth,* and for the next couple of minutes the two vessels, big and small, moved along Ambrose Channel together, while the cutter's passengers, one at a time, were lent a hand by the liner's Day Officer to help them aboard. The *Manitou* was then released, and those who had left her followed the *Elizabeth*'s officer through the ship's dimly lit but busy "working alleyway."

They passed cooks, bakers, and able seamen. Once they stepped aside for a man wheeling a large cart of fresh vegetables. Stewards carrying trays of coffee and rolls spread the smells of breakfast everywhere. A painter walked by with brushes and a pail. A stewardess followed with a pile of linen, and then came a master at arms who saluted the ship's officer. And the newcomers walked around a butcher in a bloody apron talking with a man in formal dinner dress. The alleyway led through scores of departments serving the great liner.

The men who boarded the *Queen Elizabeth* that morning went to different parts of the ship to carry out their duties in connection with the landing in New York. Had they instead kept walking, they could have continued through the immense steamship all day and into the night without retracing their steps. It is possible to walk twenty-two miles on the *Queen Elizabeth* and not cover the same piece of deck twice.

A thousand and more such facts have been used over three decades to stress that here is the world's largest liner. She is truly a superlative. She has been said to be taller, wider, heavier, more massive, more beautiful, more historic—and on and on—than any ship of her kind. Perhaps her greatest boast is that she was certainly one of the two most important ships of World War II. The *Elizabeth* and her sister ship, the *Queen Mary,* were said to have shortened the European part of the war by as much as a year. They "challenged the fury of Hitlerism in the Battle of the Atlantic," said Sir Winston Churchill. "At a speed never before realized in war, they carried a million men to defend the liberties of civilization. Often whole divisions at a time were moved by each ship. Vital decisions depended upon their ability continuously to elude the enemy, and without their aid the day of final victory must unquestionably have been postponed."

Through nearly all their history the *"Queen* Ships" have been among the most massive man-made objects to be moved by machinery. They were the first ships over a thousand feet long. The *Elizabeth,* slightly the larger, is 1,031 feet from stem to stern, 118 feet wide, and 234 feet from her keel to the top of her highest mast. She is of 82,997 gross tons, which includes a 50,000-ton hull bound together with ten million rivets. The hull encloses a self-contained community with everything necessary to keep her afloat, offer her passengers the utmost in luxury, and move her at speeds few steamships can equal. She has kitchens to feed 2,197 passengers and 1,280 crew members three times a day, and cabins to sleep them all. She has thirty-seven public rooms, some large enough to seat a convention of hundreds of people. And there are two gymnasiums, two motion picture theaters, three swimming pools, one dozen cocktail bars, a regulation squash court, and rooms that contain dog kennels, barbershops, banks, stores, steam baths, and scores of services. Yet space remains to transport enough cargo to fill every cubic inch of a large two-story house. Everything about her is big, even the whistles weighing a ton apiece, mounted on the largest smokestacks afloat.

The superlatives go on and on. No larger liners than the *Queen* Ships have been built since the day in 1938 when the *Elizabeth* was launched on Scotland's River Clyde, and the New York *Herald Tribune* reported that "Putting the *Queen Elizabeth* into the Clyde is like dumping a whale into a bathtub." Nor are such liners likely to be built in the future. The economics of ocean travel in the jet age, with the increasing costs of building and operating liners, prevent it. Thus the *Queen* Ships are unique vessels, built and operated at the peak of an historic era of immensity in ocean liners.

As she entered New York Harbor that April morning, the *Elizabeth* was completing what her logbook labeled "Voyage 423." The figure represented the number of voyages since her official maiden voyage in September 1946. However, she had actually completed many more ocean trips, for her official voyage count does not include the thousands of miles in military service between her launching in 1938 and her peacetime conversion in 1946. Nearly all her postwar voyages were made from Southampton, England, across the Channel to Cherbourg, France, and on over the North Atlantic to the Port of New York—to return then along the same route. In these hundreds of Atlantic crossings, the *Queen Elizabeth* worked with the *Queen Mary,* each traveling in opposite directions and passing in mid-Atlantic every weekend. For years the sister ships provided a weekly Atlantic express service. Nearly 2.5 million passengers had been carried on the ocean's most magnificent ferries.

But now the *Queen* Ships were near the final pages of their logbooks. In about eighteen months, as it turned out, the *Queen Mary* would be retired to Long Beach, California, where she would serve as a maritime museum and hotel. In about thirty months the *Elizabeth* would be retired in a similar role.

This book documents a voyage on one of the historic

Queen Ships. It tells about a single ocean crossing in the
Queen Elizabeth's latter days. We will follow her through the
liner's Voyage 424, beginning in New York and ending in
Southampton, England.[1] Besides learning about the *Queen*
Ships themselves, we will spend considerable time with the
Elizabeth's Master and crew as they sail the huge steamer
across the North Atlantic. And we will be party to passenger
life aboard the last of a kind of luxury liner now being left to
the past.

Actually our book starts with the landing of the *Elizabeth*
at New York's Pier 92, followed by what shippers call the
"turnaround," in which the vessel is prepared for her next
sailing. Then we will witness the "undocking," as Voyage 424
commences across the Atlantic.

By chance, our selection of Voyage 424 was all the more
interesting because it took place as an extremely bad storm
damaged and endangered ships over a great stretch of the
North Atlantic. The storm remained very much alive as the
Elizabeth set forth on Voyage 424. Indeed, the large English
liner encountered still another rough storm that damaged
ships and killed several men. Yet most of her passengers were
not greatly concerned that they were at sea during such dangerous and disruptive weather. They were forced to remain
inside much of the time, but they had a fascinating floating
city in which to roam. Keeping them safe, comfortable, and
happy while crossing such a sea at nearly 30 knots was a demanding task for men who are truly master mariners.

---

[1] Most of the *Elizabeth*'s official voyages have included the full round trip
between Southampton and New York, but 424 was a single eastward crossing
because the Bermuda cruise had temporarily changed the routine numbering
system.

Chapter 11

Up the Hudson

"All aboard from the cutter," called out the *Elizabeth*'s Junior First Officer, John K. Finlay, watching the *Manitou* from the starboard wing of the ship's flying bridge, 98 feet above the water line.

"All aboard from the cutter," repeated the Chief Quartermaster, Charles Ernest Bell, at the helm inside the *Elizabeth*'s wheelhouse.

"All aboard from the cutter," said the ship's Captain, Geoffrey Thrippleton Marr, who was standing at a forward

window of the wheelhouse overlooking the *Elizabeth*'s long
main deck and knighthead.

As the Captain repeated the announcement of the boarding, a quartermaster hoisted two small flags from the flying
bridge to the ship's forward mast. One, called an "M Flag,"
with a blue background and a white cross, signified that customs officials were now aboard. A "J Flag" with three blue
and white vertical stripes indicated that Immigration officials
were aboard. An "H Flag," with red and white vertical stripes,
was already displayed, indicating a harbor pilot was on board.
When the two new flags were in place, it was reported to the
Captain.

The Captain of the *Queen Elizabeth,* who is always the
senior member of the Cunard fleet, holds the honorary title of
Commodore of the famous shipping line. Commodore Marr,
fifty-seven years old, had only recently moved up to the fleet's
highest command position; however, he had often commanded the *Elizabeth* as a relief captain in the recent past. He
had been with Cunard since 1936, and had served frequently
as an officer in various capacities on both the *Queen* Ships.
This April morning he wore a long, dark bridge coat as he
overseered his liner's landing in New York. He walked
around the wheelhouse with determined strides and occasionally went out on the wings. There he encountered a stiff, cool
breeze ordinarily strong enough to blow off a man's hat, but
the Commodore's white-topped cap was set too tightly on his
head for such a mishap.

In the *Queen Elizabeth*'s large wheelhouse, paneled with
a dark brown wood, it was remarkably quiet, and from the
expansive row of windows the ship seemed to be gliding
slowly and effortlessly into the harbor. In the age of minia-
turization and printed circuits, the technology of the bridge
seemed extremely simple and somewhat gross—a vestige of
the machine age. Chief Quartermaster Bell was at one of the

ship's two wheels, and two other quartermasters were standing by the ship's four telegraphs which relay orders for engine settings to the two engine rooms below. The Junior Third Officer was also in the wheelhouse to make sure the various commands were clearly communicated to the right people. Two young bridge boys were on hand to answer telephones and do any other required chores. And, at the rear of the wheelhouse, were an officer from the ship's engineering department and a man from the electrical department. When any of these men on the bridge spoke to one another, they kept their voices low so as not to interfere with the commands called out by the harbor pilot and repeated by the crew. The man most relaxed of all was the Commodore, who talked with his officers and the pilot about a variety of subjects.

The pilot, Captain Robert Ahrens of the New Jersey Sandy Hook Pilots Association, was the only person on the bridge not in uniform. He wore a business suit, overcoat, and fedora. Captain Ahrens had boarded the *Elizabeth* at about 7 a.m. while the ship was still at sea. He had arrived by motor launch from the Association's pilot boat and had come aboard by climbing up a rope ladder to one of the shell doors. Now he stood at a center window in the wheelhouse where he had a broad view of the waters ahead and of the Verrazano-Narrows Bridge in the distance. He was providing the compass headings which allowed Chief Quartermaster Bell to steer the safest course up the Ambrose Channel, through the Narrows into New York's Upper Bay, and finally into the Hudson River on the west side of Manhattan Island. Near Pier 92, he would hand over the *Elizabeth* to a man from the Reynolds Pilots Association who specializes in docking large ocean liners in New York.

"Steer three-four-six," said the harbor pilot, and the number was repeated by the Chief Quartermaster, who simultaneously turned the large ship slightly to starboard. The

pilot's directions laid down the true compass heading the liner
was to follow until another figure was called out. In a few
minutes he ordered, "Steer zero-zero-two," and the Quartermaster again brought her to starboard. Thus the Sandy Hook
pilot held the *Queen Elizabeth* to the Ambrose Channel and
guided her directly through the Narrows.

Captain Ahrens also determined the ship's speed. At one
point he called out, "Half ahead!" His command, repeated
around the wheelhouse, was followed by a ringing of bells as
the quartermasters operated the ship's telegraphs and signaled
the *Elizabeth*'s forward and after engine rooms, more than ten
decks below, to reduce revolutions on her four large propellers from 100 to 80 per minute. This slowed her from 17 to 13
knots.

Before Captain Ahrens had boarded the ship, Commodore Marr had ordered his engineers onto "maneuvering
revs." Under these orders the engine department works with
the understanding that "Full Ahead" on the telegraphs estab-
lishes 100 revolutions as the propellers' maximum speed. A
higher maximum is used at sea when "Full Ahead" calls for
about 170 revolutions to push the ship around 28 knots, depending on the weather. But in confined harbor waters, the
lower maximum revolutions (sometimes called "harbor
revs") holds the liner down to a safer, more reasonable speed.

The low speed in New York Harbor is a crucial rule of
the road for the *Elizabeth*. Of course, it is important should
the ship have to stop quickly, but there are other reasons.
Ambrose Channel in places is as shallow as 44 feet—which
leaves little clearance to spare with 40 feet of the *Queen Elizabeth*'s hull below the water line. The lack of depth could
lead such a large vessel to serious difficulties should she move
too fast. With too much speed her stern drags down, and her
hull piles up water underneath and to the front. The increased pressure upon the liner's bottom can then play havoc

with the steering. She might, in the words of a seaman, "take a run," or "sheer." The ship that takes a run actually veers to one side, though the rudder is trying to hold her straight ahead. No pilot can afford to take a run with the *Queen Elizabeth* because her length and mass allow little room for side excursions in New York Harbor.

Another reason for the *Elizabeth*'s taking it easy is that she leaves more wash than any other steamship. In New York Harbor it could damage boats and dock facilities along the shores of Manhattan, Brooklyn, New Jersey, and Staten Island. Swimmers on Coney Island beaches have often been surprised by the unusually high surf created by the *Elizabeth* as she headed toward Ambrose.

"Pilot," said Commodore Marr to Captain Ahrens, "when did you come out?" He meant when had the pilot left his home to come out to the Sandy Hook Association's 215-foot pilot boat on station near the Ambrose Lightship. Here the pilots who guide practically all ships entering and leaving New York Harbor wait for their inbound assignments. When it's a man's turn to go to work, he is delivered to his ship by a 40-foot motor launch.

"I came out last night," said Captain Ahrens. "Just finished my days off."

"Are we your first ship in?" asked the Commodore.

"Yes," said the pilot. "I had a good night's rest and here I am."

Captain Ahrens and about a hundred and forty other Sandy Hook pilots work at one of the most ancient occupations connected with the sea. Since men have sailed to foreign lands they have needed pilots in the unknown and dangerous waters at the mouth of a safe harbor. "A shift in the wind before a reef without a pilot," says a history of the venerable profession, "and the spices of India could lie deep at the mouth of the harbor. A storm off the coast of Dover without a

pilot could bereave the most prominent homes of England."
In the earliest days of Colonial America, Sandy Hook, a long
thin extension of New Jersey's northernmost seacoast, was the
vantage point from which pilots met incoming ships. But
highly competitive bar pilots raced each other to the best ships
for the most lucrative work. Meanwhile other inbound vessels
might never see a pilot. The free-for-all system was also unfair
to the pilots themselves because they sailed many a useless
mile for jobs that never materialized. Pilotage therefore lent
itself to the formation of an association that could apportion
the work fairly, and the Sandy Hook organization became one
of the most important in the world.

The fact that Captain Ahrens could pilot the *Queen Elizabeth* indicated he had risen to the top of his profession. To
learn his trade he first had to serve seven years as an appren-
tice. Meanwhile he had to pass stringent examinations. He
knew by heart every detail of the New York and New Jersey
harbor waters, including the bottom surface, rocks, reefs,
shoals, buoys, and currents. With such facts in his head, he was
then allowed to progress slowly from the smallest vessels
entering the harbor to the largest.

With the slow steaming called for by Captain Ahrens, it
took the *Queen* Ship one hour to travel the dozen miles from
the Ambrose Lightship to the Verrazano-Narrows Bridge. As
she sailed ever so slowly toward the beautiful steel arch over
the Narrows, it appeared that her masts might hit the bridge.
The masts are the highest structures to pass under the Verrazano Bridge, but they miss the underside by 33 feet at mean
high water.

"Steer zero-zero-nine," commanded the pilot as the *Elizabeth* came out of the Narrows. The new heading brought her
to starboard, slightly to the northeast and into the Upper Bay.

From the Verrazano Bridge to Pier 92 took another hour

of slow steaming. The main channel in that ten miles ranges
from 45 to 55 feet in depth, and as it leads up into the Hudson
River, the distance to the surrounding shores decreases.
Therefore Captain Ahrens continued reducing the liner's
speed because of the increased possibility of wash damage.

"Slow ahead!" he said at one point, and revolutions were
reduced to 60 per minute, delivering a speed of only ten
knots. Once in the Hudson River, Captain Ahrens called out,
"Dead slow ahead!" and the revolutions were cut back to 40
per minute (seven knots).

From high on the liner's bridge her forward motion was
now almost imperceptible. But on a lovely April morning,
coming up the Bay and into the Hudson, few of the *Elizabeth's* passengers and crew cared about speed. Before them
was one of the most majestic sights on earth, the towers of
lower Manhattan that form the famous New York skyline.
Hundreds of passengers had eaten their breakfast and were
crowding the starboard decks from which they could look over
into the busy city. At the same time tens of thousands of
people were watching the *Elizabeth* from Manhattan office
windows in the downtown financial district. A *Queen* Ship
can hardly slip into New York Harbor unnoticed.

While excitement was evident among the passengers, who
busily and noisily pointed out the sights to one another, the
men on the bridge betrayed few of the same feelings. Though
none of them can enter the Harbor of New York guiding the
world's largest liner without feelings of pride and excitement,
it remained unusually silent on the sun-bathed navigation
bridge as the great buildings of Manhattan seemed to move
slowly along the starboard beam.

Commodore Marr broke the silence as a Circle Line sightseeing boat sailed by, and her passengers waved at the people
on the *Elizabeth*. The Commodore walked out to the port

wing, looked down on the small boat, and commented: "They are getting a bonus today with the *Queen Elizabeth* coming in."

When the ship had arrived at a point in the river almost in line with the Empire State Building, Junior First Officer Finlay called out, "Docking pilot on board!" A tugboat owned by the Moran Towing and Transportation Company had just sailed out from a New York pier and delivered the new pilot to a shell door on the liner. He soon walked into the wheelhouse, reported to Commodore Marr, shook hands with the Sandy Hook pilot, and then took over the pilotage for the complex job of docking the immense liner.

Captain Ahrens in the past couple of hours had earned a fee of $400. Sandy Hook pilots are paid $10 per foot of draft for bringing a vessel in or out of New York Harbor. The *Elizabeth,* with its 40-foot draft, called for the highest fee listed on the pilotage rate card. The money would be paid by the Cunard Company to the association whose members would then share it. Though Captain Ahrens brought in the largest liner in the world that morning, he would receive the same amount as a member with comparable standing piloting a boat with only a six-foot draft for a $60 fee.

Captain Ahrens left the bridge and went below for coffee. When the *Elizabeth* docked he would go to his office in lower Manhattan for another assignment, perhaps on a ship leaving New York.

Chapter III

Docking

The docking pilot was Captain Barney Scherer, a member of the Reynolds Pilots Association, an organization of highly skilled pilots who specialize in docking large ships in New York. They are associated with the 103-year-old Moran Towing and Transportation Company, America's most famous tugboat company. Captain Scherer is one of only six pilots qualified to dock the two *Queen* Ships in New York, and to him they are liners unlike all others. "They're the greatest ships to handle as far as our end of the business is concerned.

You wonder how you can move so much metal so well. You can stop engines down at Twenty-third Street and steer them under their own way right off Fiftieth Street. If this weren't true, it would be impossible to handle such big ships. Most other liners we bring in are very light. In the wind you have to be careful. But the wind doesn't affect the *Queens* very much. They are so deep and heavy. If I had a choice of steady work all year on liners, I would take the *Queens*."

"We're a little ahead of time this morning," Commodore Marr said to Captain Scherer, who was already giving orders determining the ship's speed and direction.

"It's good to be early this time of year," said the docking pilot, who speaks with a pronounced New York accent, in sharp contrast to the Commodore's cultivated, British speech that one might associate with an English country gentleman. "We've got freshets coming down the river," continued Captain Scherer. "Snow melting up in the mountains this time of year."

The freshets could seriously effect the tides, which are important to docking a *Queen* Ship in New York. A docking can occur on either the two low water slack periods, or the two high water slacks—all of which result from the two natural tidal changes every 24 hours. Commodore Marr prefers low water slack because the incoming liner then stems the down-river current of the ebbing tide, and she steers easily. To bring her in with a flood tide's up-river current on her stern makes steering more difficult. According to the tide tables for that April 12th, low water slack should occur at the moment Captain Scherer had maneuvered the *Elizabeth* around at a right angle to the Hudson opposite Pier 92 and pointed her directly into the slip. At slack water the river's tidal movement would stop briefly, and the ship would be free of sidewise pressure. Then the pilot would have to concern himself only with the ship's forward movement under her own power.

When the maneuver is well timed with the tides, the docking is done with comparative ease and the greatest safety. But freshets make tidal timing unpredictable, and they worry docking pilots.

As the *Elizabeth* passed Forty-second Street, five more tugboats joined the one that had delivered Captain Scherer, and they distributed themselves along the black hull. Seamen from the decks above heaved small lines down to the tugs' deckhands, who tied them to large ropes coiled neatly on the decks of the small boats. The lines were then used to haul the heavy ropes up the tall sides of the ship. Each rope, six inches in diameter, required the strength of several men to haul it up onto the *Elizabeth,* but in a few minutes all the tugs were made fast to the liner. The ropes were not to be used for towing the big ship, but were simply to keep the six small boats and the liner together as the large vessel sailed on up the river.

When the tugs were made fast to the *Queen Elizabeth* the fact was announced by Junior First Officer Finlay. Though he was unable to see all the boats from his station on the flying bridge, he was in radio communication by walkie-talkie with officers who could see them. Finlay could talk with the ship's Staff Captain, John Storey, on the stern in the "docking bridge," and with the Chief Officer, Victor Arbuckle, forward on the "knighthead." Both officers could look over the liner's sides to observe the tugs near their quarters of the ship.

For the next few minutes, the *Elizabeth* dragged the tugs toward the pier at Fifty-second Street. Meanwhile Captain Scherer called out orders to the liner's quartermasters when he wanted her steered to port or starboard, or when he wanted engine changes.

"Hard a-starboard!" ordered the docking pilot. The Chief Quartermaster, repeating the command, turned the ship's wheel several revolutions clockwise while watching a

large dial in front of him, the "rudder indicator," on which a
pointer revealed that the ship's 140-ton rudder was turning to
starboard as far as it could go. The vessel barely responded,
for at "Dead Slow Ahead," seven knots, the rudder had only a
slight effect on her course.

Like the ship's officers, Captain Scherer also used a walkie-
talkie to communicate with the various tugboat captains down
around the water line. They were addressed by their boats'
first names drawn from members of the Moran family, past or
present. One tug at the side of the *Queen Elizabeth* was the
Nancy Moran, so Captain Scherer addressed her captain
simply as "the *Nancy*."

While the large liner turned ever so slowly to starboard,
still proceeding up the river, Captain Scherer ordered his six
tugboats into their working positions. They arranged themselves in teams and the docking pilot needed to address only
one tug of a team to have all respond. On the starboard bow,
Captain Scherer had four tugs turn abreast of one another at
right angles to the ship. The remaining two tugs were ordered
to do the same on the starboard quarter. All six tugboats
pressed their bows, heavily padded with large rubber bump-
ers, against the riveted steel sides of the ship, while their captains waited for radio orders from the pilot.

But staying at right angles to a liner moving forward
demands a tugboat captain's skill acquired from many years'
experience—and a very special ship. Most ships, to be steered,
have to be moving through the water, but a tugboat, which
spends a large part of her life pressing against objects that
hardly move at all, must be steerable while practically standing still. When the object, in this instance the *Queen Elizabeth,* is sliding sidewise across the direction in which a tug is
pushing, the difficulties are magnified. Then it is extremely
tricky to maintain a right angle to the large vessel and con-

tinuously capitalize on the small boat's power.

This problem, peculiar to a tugboat, is solved by a powerful engine far out of proportion to the size of the vessel. For example, one of the tugs beside the *Elizabeth* that morning had a 1,750 horsepower diesel engine, powerful enough for a large cargo ship. The engine whirled a five-bladed propeller nine feet in diameter—extremely big for the vessel it drives. The long blades, designed for power rather than speed, take a heavy bite of water with each turn. They therefore produce an extra large amount of quick water which flows directly back across a big rudder immediately to the rear and center of the blades. This force against the moving rudder can swing the tugboat's stern left or right, though she is making little headway.

As the *Queen Elizabeth* came within a city block of Cunard's pier, her rudder was beginning to bring the liner around to a right angle with the river and headed into the slip. But this meant that her stern had to be forced out into the downstream flow of the ebbing tide, and the liner's rudder alone could by no means do the job. So help was needed. Captain Scherer called for it from two sources: from the tugs and from the liner's engines.

First he went to the tugs for help. The team of four pushing on the starboard bow acted as a pivot on which to hold the forward end of the great ship from swinging southward. Meanwhile the two tugs astern pushed with all their power to move the ship's stern up river against the tide.

"Full ahead on the *Moira!*" ordered the docking pilot over his radio. The captain of the *Moira Moran,* down on the *Elizabeth*'s starboard quarter, acknowledged with two shrill toots of his "regulation whistle," used by tug captains for fast, convenient communication over short distances. The *Moira* with a sister tug beside her began pushing as hard as their power plants allowed. The roar of the engines increased, and quick water churned the river as the two small boats shoved hard on the big ship.

At the same time Captain Scherer called for the tugboats near the starboard bow to step up their power. "One bell ahead on the *Nancy!*" commanded the pilot. Back came the sharp acknowledgment of a double toot. The engines of all four forward tugs picked up speed, and the Hudson River was filled with the rumble of diesels as they helped swing the *Elizabeth* against the flow of the ebbing tide.

Captain Scherer then quickly turned to his second source of power, the liner's engines. "Half astern two starboard!" he called out to the men in the wheelhouse. They repeated the command as two quartermasters telegraphed the engine rooms to reverse the liner's two starboard propellers at 80 revolutions per minute. Meanwhile, the two port propellers were kept going in the forward direction, though their speed, by another order from Captain Scherer, was increased to "Half Ahead" (80 revolutions).

Now the propellers on the ship's opposing sides were turning in opposite directions, and they exerted a twisting force upon the liner's hull. In other words, the port propellers pushed forward on the ship's left side while those on the starboard pulled backward on the right side—all of which had the tendency to swing the vessel's stern to the left, and up the river.

Despite all the force of the six tugboats plus the ship's four sets of steam turbines that can develop 160,000 horsepower, the movement of the liner was barely perceptible. No man-made force is likely to move a mass such as the *Queen Elizabeth* in a great hurry under any circumstances. When the tide, striking with full force upon one long side of the liner, is in opposition, it's a wonder that she can be moved at all.

Commodore Marr was not directly or actively involved in

this docking operation, though clearly he was most concerned about it. "The ship is always under the master's command," he explained, "and the pilot is here to advise. A pilot is never able to assume full responsibility. You must have a captain in command, and the captain has the authority to countermand the pilot's orders. Actually one tends to leave it to the pilot when one feels he is doing what he should. Any time the pilot was endangering the ship it would be the master's duty to say, 'All right, pilot, I will carry on.' "

As the *Queen Elizabeth* was being docked that April morning, Captain Scherer remained very much in charge. While her stern slowly swung to the north in the Hudson River, and four tugs kept her bow from going south, the docking pilot continually called out orders that applied the right amount of push from the tugs, or the correct degree of twist from the engines of the 83,000-ton liner.

But as the minutes passed, the pilot's concern about the spring freshets increased. The river neither looked nor felt right to Captain Scherer, who has worked on the Hudson for twenty-seven years. The down-river current against the ship persisted when it should be abating, and the tugboats had difficulty bringing the liner completely abreast of the river.

Commodore Marr sensed the lack of progress and walked from the starboard wing through the wheelhouse to the port wing where he could look north at the river. He saw that it was still unusually active for low water slack. Then the Commodore suddenly glanced back over the liner's superstructure and sighted upon a point on the New Jersey shore. This confirmed, as he had sensed, that the ship's stern was commencing to swing ever so slowly back to the south. He looked somewhat concerned until he had walked back to the wheelhouse and learned from Captain Scherer that the change in direction was a result of the pilot's decision, not the river taking control of the liner.

Captain Scherer had ordered the *Moira Moran* and her partner to allow the *Elizabeth*'s stern to swing back down the Hudson to align the vessel with the persistent current. "We'll hold her here until things settle down a bit," explained the docking pilot. "You can't predict with these spring freshets on a river running hundreds of miles from up north. You get melting snows pouring water in from the mountains upstate, and naturally they're going to affect the river. By this time we should have gone through the slack, and the tide should be moving up the river."

The tugboats slowly eased the *Queen Elizabeth*'s stern around until she was almost directly across the slip between the Cunard pier and the parallel Italian Line pier immediately to the south. At that point one could look down upon the roof of the nearby pier from the starboard wing of the *Elizabeth*'s flying bridge, which projects over the ship's sides. Below, the six Moran tugs were still noisily churning the waters as they held the large liner from bumping the pier. Meanwhile, Captain Scherer inched the *Elizabeth* forward to position her bow just slightly off the Cunard pier almost directly ahead.

As the liner moved forward, Commodore Marr requested via the ship's walkie-talkies that Chief Officer Arbuckle on the knighthead keep the bridge informed of the distance to the pier ahead. "One-zero-three feet," replied the Chief Officer, and he kept reporting in this way until the liner was stopped and held some 60 feet off the pier.

The Chief Officer's guidance was needed because it is difficult from high on the bridge to judge distance between the bow and nearby objects. "Fortunately things look closer than they are," explained Commodore Marr. "It's like backing your car out of the garage. When it looks as though the fender were about to touch the side of the door, you know you still have a few feet to spare. When it looks from the bridge as though the ship were about to touch the pier we still have fifty feet to go."

Commodore Marr was most concerned that the ship's bow did not touch the pier ahead. A touch from the *Queen Elizabeth,* even the least bit out of control, could cause a serious amount of damage. One time the liner gently nudged her New York pier by accident and left a $20,000 repair job.

"It may look to you," the Commodore said, "as if she is landing extremely gently, but if she has any run on at all, it is like hitting the pier with a heavy-headed hammer weighing 83,000 tons."

If the destructive force of a *Queen* Ship at a creep is a serious matter, consider what one could do with her power let out on the high seas. It was demonstrated during World War II when the 450-foot cruiser the *Curacao* accidentally cut across the bows of the *Queen Mary* as she was steaming at a top speed over the North Atlantic not far from Scotland. The *Mary,* loaded with American G.I.'s and under orders not to stop or slow down for any reason, hit the *Curacao* about eleven feet from her stern. The 4,200-ton escort cruiser carrying 439 officers and ratings was flipped over and then, directly in line with the oncoming *Queen,* she was cut, crushed, and twisted by the liner's extremely strong bows. In seconds the Royal Navy lost 338 men. Bound by her orders never to stop and thereby increase her exposure to an enemy torpedo, the *Mary* continued, while two other naval vessels picked up survivors—the cruiser's captain, one officer, and 99 ratings. The liner's prow was buckled. However, the damage was not so serious and temporary repairs in Scotland allowed her to return with a load of servicemen to America for more permanent repairs. The event was held a close secret until the end of the war.

Captain Scherer held the *Elizabeth* for nearly fifteen minutes cocked between the British and Italian Line piers

while he waited for the river currents to abate. Finally, he
could see that slack water was truly beginning, so the docking
pilot started calling out commands. "Full ahead on the
Moira!" he ordered, and from the distance came the high-
pitched toots of acknowledgment. He then called for more
power from the team of tugs led by the *Nancy*.

The slip was filled with their roar, and once more the
Elizabeth was swung slowly around into the Hudson with her
stern moving slowly to the north. This time the effect of the
spring freshets was nearly spent, and the tugboats with the
help of the liner's engines were able to bring the ship abreast
of the river.

As the maneuver ended—according to Captain Scherer's
calculation—the current stopped in the Hudson, and for a
few moments the river was like a calm lake. The docking pilot
ordered a general reduction of power from his tugs, which he
then used only for a few comparatively gentle nudges to help
position the mammoth liner more precisely in line with the
side of the pier whose outer end was now on the *Elizabeth*'s
port bow.

Simultaneously Captain Scherer directed the ship's crew
to stop two of the liner's engines, one on each side. Then he
ordered that the two remaining propellers proceed at dead
slow ahead (40 revolutions) and the *Queen Elizabeth* moved
forward, at a barely perceptible speed, toward the pier where
she was to tie up.

Indeed, on this last few feet of her voyage, the pilot made
sure the liner's speed was kept to the absolute minimum. Not
only was he concerned about stopping the liner at the proper
point, but he was most concerned about not roiling up the
water in the slip ahead. As the *Queen Elizabeth* moved into
the comparatively small opening between the British and Italian Line piers, the vessel's displacement would force a great
deal of water out of the slip. Should this happen too fast, the

displaced water rushing out into the Hudson could cause such turbulence that it could possibly damage small craft in the area.

"Now she is sliding beautifully," said Commodore Marr, obviously relieved that they had come through the minor bout with the spring freshets unscathed. Captain Scherer nodded, smiled a bit, but continued concentrating upon the movement of the ship toward her stopping place.

If for some reason this docking maneuver has to be done at high water slack, the tugs are placed on the port side rather than starboard. Instead of pushing the ship around, they allow the upstream force of the tide to move her—with her bow as a pivot and the stern swinging up river—until the great ship is abreast of the Hudson. The tugs' power is then used simply to keep the liner under control, to insure that the currents do not carry her too far. Once at a right angle to the Hudson, the liner is aligned with the slip until slack water, then in she goes.

Commodore Marr's immediate predecessor, Commodore Frederick George Watts, holds the distinction of berthing the *Queen* several times when tugboats were unavailable because of a strike. Commodore Watts used the upriver currents produced by the flood tide for power to help maneuver the liner. The ship's bow was carefully brought up to the outer end of the Cunard pier until she gently touched. Then the pier was used as a pivot to hold the ship's bow while the current swung her stern out into and up the river. But it was a matter of split second timing, using the engines and the last moments of the flood tide, to stop this swing as the ship was at right angles to the river at exactly high water slack when she could steam directly forward into the slip. As he made these landings, Commodore Watts called for nearly a hundred engine maneuvers to change the speed and direction of the vessel's four large propellers. On one of the tugless landings the master had to contend with a 30-knot wind and 16-degree weather. It was during one of these landings that the *Elizabeth* accidentally dealt $20,000 damage to the pier.

"In a situation like that," said Commodore Watts, "you haven't much time to think about things like damaging a flag-pole. Your concentration has to be one hundred percent on getting the ship into the dock. If you do real damage you can cost your company thousands of pounds in missed sailings."

On that lovely day in April when Captain Scherer was docking the *Queen Elizabeth,* he moved the liner slowly alongside the pier with no more delay. Meanwhile her officers all moved to the port wing where they could look down upon two men in a rowboat, mosquito-sized compared to the giant ship, rowing out to meet the *Queen Elizabeth.* These men, always the delight of dockside photographers, have been nick-named "Peter and Paul," which seems to have no bearing on their task of catching the first line dropped from the ship. Once it was in their hands Peter and Paul rowed back to the dock where the line was used to pull in the first of many heavy ropes that would be used to make the ship fast.

As the liner slid along the pier, the officers and docking pilot on the flying bridge were at eye level with the top of a steel superstructure supported by the building below. Along the top of this structure were three upright rods, each labeled with the name of a Cunard ship. First was the *Caronia,* then the *Queen Mary,* and finally the *Queen Elizabeth.* These rods serve as guides so that each ship can be precisely docked in order that the pier's large, heavy gangways fit the vessel's doors. On the *Elizabeth*'s port wing an inch-wide red line is painted on the outer railing, and when she is docked in New York, the line must be exactly opposite her rod atop the pier. For the gangways to fit, the 1,031-foot steamship cannot be even six inches off the mark—all of which is not easily accomplished.

As the liner crept to its designated marker, dockworkers below were dragging line after line ashore to tie up the ship, for it takes ten large hawsers to make the *Queen Elizabeth* fast to her pier. From the forward deck two "head ropes" stretch out to the pier ahead of the bow. Two more ropes, the "forward backsprings," cross the head ropes, angling back to the pier some distance behind the bow. On the stern a similar arrangement of four ropes cross each other in pairs. One pair, the "stern ropes," stretch out to the ship's rear, while the other pair, the "after backsprings," are made fast to the pier somewhat forward of the stern. On the ship's deck all these ropes are wrapped around electrically driven capstans, which can apply tension to make final adjustments to the ship's position during a docking.

When these ropes were made fast on the pier, the officers on the *Elizabeth*'s forward and afterdecks radioed the bridge.

"Stop engines!" ordered Commodore Marr who had taken over from the docking pilot. The Commodore stood on the bridge wing directly in front of the red line.

"Three-zero feet!" he called out as the line was an estimated 30 feet from the *Elizabeth*'s marker rod.

Each time the Commodore's words were repeated around the bridge by the officers and quartermasters.

"Two-zero feet ahead!"

"Stand by to check all the backsprings."

"Slow astern starboard!" Now he was once more using two of the propellers to brake the ship and force her stern toward the pier as she slid forward to her mark.

"Hold everything forward."

"Six inches to go ahead!"

"Hold on forward! Hold on aft!" These commands to

"hold on" were relayed to deck hands operating the capstans that then tightened the ropes to help stop the ship.

"Two feet astern!" The liner had now passed her mark by 24 inches.

"Three feet astern!"

"Heave on the backsprings!" With this order the forward backsprings were hauled in by capstans to stop the ship and drag her backwards. Still her momentum, even at a creep, kept her going ahead.

"Four feet astern!"

"Six feet astern!"

"Half astern starboard!" Now, decided the Commodore, he needed more than ropes, so he called for a speed-up in reverse of the starboard propellers. And that did the job.

"Hold on forward! Hard!"

"Two feet astern!" She was now moving back.

"One foot astern!"

"Stop starboard!"

"Hold the headlines!"

"Hold on aft!"

"Hold everything! Hold *hard* on everything!"

"In position! Make fast!"

With this final command, Commodore Marr turned dramatically, walked back through the wheelhouse and then down to his private quarters directly under the navigation bridge.

The last two lines, the "breast ropes," were slowly drawn up. They stretch from the ship straight out across the other sets of ropes, one fore, one aft, to pull the ship directly toward the pier. When this was done, the *Elizabeth*'s hull at the water line was pressing against several large wooden rafts (fenders) that keep the ship and pier from touching directly. These last fine adjustments to the ship were directed by Captain Nigel A. F. Kingscote, Cunard's Marine Superintendent at Pier 92.

He stood on the open end of the gangway for first-class passengers to make sure it was centered exactly upon the port door to which it would attach.

When the liner finally came to a rest, she was stopped in one of the very few berths in the world that can take a *Queen* Ship. In addition to New York, only nine other ports can berth one of the *Queens:* Southampton, Cherbourg, Capetown, Las Palmas (Canary Islands), Palma (Majorca), San Francisco, Cristobal, Long Beach, and Vancouver.

It was the end of Voyage 423. The passengers, fresh from their Bermuda cruise, filled the gangways that had been rolled into place and began the chore of passing customs inspection in the large shedlike pier. Before landing they had all been cleared for entry into the United States by the U.S. Immigration and Public Health officials who had met the ship aboard the Coast Guard cutter *Manitou.*

While the passengers were disembarking, hundreds of crew members remaining aboard the *Elizabeth* were already preparing the liner for her 424th voyage.

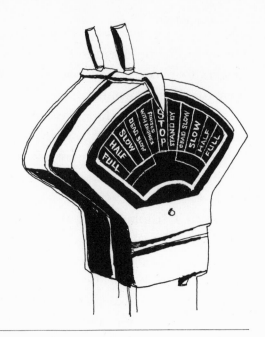

Chapter I V

Turnaround

After the docking, Commodore Marr enjoyed a lunch served in the main room of his quarters by Rowland Hill, his personal valet, traditionally known as the "Captain's Tiger." The Commodore sat at one side of the room at a small table always supplied with a bowl of fresh fruit. The quarters, which include an adjoining bedroom, have a row of windows at the forward side. They overlook the *Elizabeth*'s main deck, as do a parallel set on the navigation bridge directly above. The interior walls of the quarters, hung with a few paintings and

several photographs of the *Elizabeth* and the *Mary,* are beautifully paneled in rock elm sawn from the piles of London's
original Waterloo Bridge. The elm is a light gray—bleached
by the tidal waters of the River Thames from 1811 until 1936
when the piles were replaced. On the side of the room opposite the dining table stands a small desk neatly stacked with
papers where the man responsible for the *Elizabeth* works
whenever he finds the opportunity during the busy hours of a
voyage. In the room's center is a circle of easy chairs used at
sea for frequent meetings with the ship's officers and for invited passengers entertained by the Commodore at cocktails
nearly every evening before he goes to dinner in the first-class
restaurant.

This afternoon, following lunch, Commodore Marr
spent an hour meeting with New York officials of the Cunard
Line. When they were finished, he put on a civilian business
suit, gave his valet a telephone number at which he could be
reached in emergency during the night, and left the ship. In
fifteen minutes the Master of the *Queen Elizabeth* was on a
commuter train for Greenwich, Connecticut, to visit old
friends.

Back on the liner most of the crew remained aboard, and
some were busier than they are at sea as they hurried through
the turnaround for Voyage 424. A turnaround ordinarily
takes at least 24 hours, but on pressing occasions the time has
been cut drastically, the record being 16 hours and 25 minutes.

Before Voyage 424 could begin, many things had to be
done. Mail and cargo had to be unloaded and a new batch
reloaded for delivery in Europe. The entire ship had to be
cleaned and made ready in a thousand ways for the passengers
who would board the following morning. The enormousness
of the task is pointed up when you consider that in a typical
sailing the liner uses 15,000 bed sheets and pillow slips, 12,000

tablecloths, 40,000 hand and face towels, 18,000 bath towels, and on and on. All the soiled linens had to be trucked to a laundry where a clean supply was waiting to be returned to the ship. A double supply of linen, incidentally, is shared by the *Queen* Ships. In both New York and Southampton, fresh linen for the *Elizabeth* was last week's soiled linen from the *Mary*, and vice versa. The continual swapping is possible most of the time because each vessel arrives in New York or Southampton on alternate weeks.

While the last tugboat was gathering in her lines after the *Elizabeth* was made fast at 11 a.m. that morning, a heavily loaded oil barge was towed alongside the ocean liner. The oil company's crew immediately connected hoses into several of the liner's "filling stations," and in a few minutes they were supplying the ship's tanks with the beginning of 7,000 tons of heavy, black "bunker C," a low-grade petroleum product that the *Elizabeth*'s boilers were designed to burn efficiently. Bunker C, which varies in price (about $24 a ton) from place to place, is usually cheapest in New York, so the ship's Chief Engineer arrives there as close as possible to the minimum safe level of a two-day reserve. As much as two million gallons of oil, enough to fill some two hundred railroad tank cars, has been pumped into the *Elizabeth* during a turnaround.

As the oil barge came alongside, sea water was pouring from the *Queen Elizabeth*'s starboard side because the ship's carpenter, John Bradley, was carrying out the Chief Officer's orders for ballasting the liner. This job meant loading her with fresh water and oil so she would be in balance and down in the water where she is designed to sail best. When "down to her marks," fully ballasted, the *Elizabeth* rides with the full 40 feet of her long hull below the water line. As she sails for Europe, oil is consumed at about a thousand tons a day, and water at about two thousand tons a day. By the third day at sea the liner is up out of the water several feet, and Bradley starts ballasting with seawater, judiciously pumped into her empty tanks. Back in port, therefore, the sea water has to be removed to make room for the oil and fresh water required on the forthcoming trip. During the turnaround for Voyage 424, Bradley emptied some 1,500 tons of saltwater ballast from the *Elizabeth* and arranged to pump in fresh water from the pier.

By mid-afternoon at Pier 92 deliveries, mostly of perishable foods, were being made in quantity to store the ship for Voyage 424. Though it was April, and the chill of winter remained in the New York air, the *Queen Elizabeth* was receiving watermelons and fresh strawberries to serve during the next five days at sea. The strawberries, on sale only in New York's most exclusive markets and restaurants, had come by air from California, while the watermelons had been trucked from Florida. They would be served with delicious South African plums obtained in Europe before the liner left Southampton. Other delivery trucks came with large bluefish, Maine lobster, oysters, clams, and other varieties of fresh seafood, all of which were hauled into the liner over small escalators spanning the gap between the pier and the ship.

Actually the biggest job of storing other than perishables is reserved for Southampton; still, New York purchases are made when prices are better in the United States, or when the ship requires something available only in America. "We are in the fortunate position of being able to do our housekeeping in the most advantageous market," explains Commodore Marr who, as Master, maintains a lively interest even in the most minute details of the storing job. "The Chief Steward gets a list of prices from England and the States, and judging from quality and costs, he can do his shopping so as to get the best for the best price. Sometimes potatoes are cheaper in England, sometimes in the United States."

Shopping for the *Queen Elizabeth* is always complicated

by the special demands that naturally exist among as many as two thousand passengers, many of whom pay a handsome sum not only for transportation, but for the luxuries of kings and queens. The Cunard Steam-Ship Company Limited has thus become one of the world's largest purchasers of caviar, Nova Scotia salmon, and other delicacies. The passengers also demand the finest of table wines; therefore, deep in the *Queen Elizabeth,* at a point as free as possible from the ship's movements, is a fabulous wine cellar with a hundred different selections. In addition the ship's catering specialists are prepared to take care of many unusual requests.

"From experience," says John Bainbridge, the company's assistant catering superintendent, "we know that some film star has a passion for, shall we say, some brand of English pork sausage that he gets at the Savoy in London. And we know he always asks for this on board.

"I'm thinking of a man now—a most critical man on soft fruits. You can rest assured that when a *Queen* Ship sails with him aboard that we have scoured the market for the soft fruit he desires—plums, pears, grapes, mangoes, apricots, and the like. They're the fruits with short seasons, but no matter what time of year, we go all out to get them for this gentleman.

"Another problem of this day and age is the diet. America is very diet-conscious. We have this business of cholesterol conditions and other problems calling for special foods. Before a ship sails we often receive special diet sheets telling us exactly what this or that person wants because he is on a diet. There may be twenty different dieters on the ship. But we do everything possible to supply whatever the passengers desire. It has always been a boast of ours. We often have to send to special shops in London, Paris, New York, or elsewhere to meet the requests. They'll want special gravies, special grapefruits, even very special baby foods—not for babies but for adults on special diets.

"One lady's diet sheet included a special brand of sugar-less apple juice, a natural grape juice both red and white, unsweetened pineapple juice, and corn-oil margarine—for breakfast. For lunch she called for washed grated carrots, cabbage, celery, watercress, beet root, cucumbers with the rind on, parsley, tomatoes, radishes, olive oil, lemon juice, cottage cheese made only with skim milk, and plain Cheddar cheese. We had to make sure that all these items were on board as the *Queen* sailed."

Perhaps the most demanding customer of all was a well-known woman who sailed on the *Queen Mary* years ago accompanied by her own live chickens. Her flock was kept on the boat deck near the ship's kennels, and the hens' output was rushed to the chef to meet the lady's urge to eat none other than strictly fresh eggs.

The *Queen Elizabeth*, as is true of the *Mary*, even includes, along with all of her massive cooking facilities, a complete kosher kitchen with its own chef. The food is served in a separate dining-room area with its own waiters, silverware, and dishes. In New York the ship is met by a special kosher supplier who, during the turnaround for Voyage 424, delivered some 200 pounds of beef ribs, 24 cartons of biscuit matzoh, special kosher breads, 24 large cans of pickled cucumbers, 60 pounds of kosher cheese, 100 pounds of chicken, 100 ducks, 100 fowl, gefüllte fish, calves' liver, kosher ice cream, margarine, and special cooking oil.

When the *Queen Elizabeth* is finally supplied in full to travel the Atlantic an inventory reveals that she is carrying about three thousand different items, from altar candles, wines, and communion bread, to furniture cream, safety matches, and boot polish, to deodorant blocks, floor wax, birthday candles, and cocktail sticks.

The turnaround for Voyage 424 continued through the night and was still in progress as daylight came on the 13th of

April. It was a far different day from when the *Elizabeth* arrived, for now the weather was cold and drizzly, and heavy gray clouds hovered over New York's skyscrapers, the effects of a low-pressure area moving up the East Coast from Cape Hatteras. This storm would proceed out across Nantucket Island and over the sea—along with the *Queen Elizabeth,* which was sailing at noon.

One of the early morning New Haven commuter trains carried Commodore Marr into Grand Central Station from Greenwich. Like hundreds of thousands of others going to work, the Master of the world's largest liner walked through the station to an exit where he caught a taxicab to Pier 92.

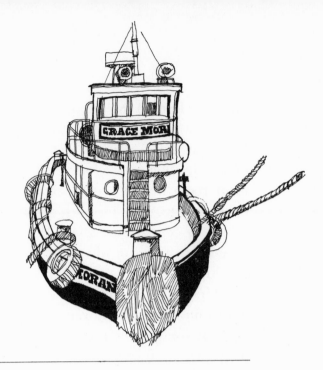

Chapter V

Voyage 424:
Embarkation and
Undocking

Embarkation for the *Queen Elizabeth*'s Voyage 424 began officially at 9 a.m., April 13. On the street in front of the Cunard pier, scores of taxicabs started delivering passengers who arrived with tons of luggage. Dockworkers, wearing red jackets supplied by Cunard, crowded around the taxis as the passengers and luggage were discharged and insistent New York policemen waved the empty cabs away to make room for more. The dockworkers carried the luggage into the pier for delivery to the ship's stewards as the passengers rode escalators up to the level of the ship's gangways.

That morning, 1,311 passengers came to Pier 92 with at least that many relatives and friends to say good-bye. They came single file up the long escalator into the huge, cavernous main room of the 1,100-foot pier where they found three ticket booths, one for each passenger class of travel: first, cabin, or tourist. Gangways for each of these classes were located according to where the accommodations are found in the ship.

First-class passengers, who have the largest, most luxurious cabins, ride in the center, primarily on three decks directly above the liner's huge first-class dining room. The cabin passengers, who pay somewhat less, ride on the decks just aft of first class. And the tourist passengers, with the least expensive cabins, are forward of first class. The possible price range for a *Queen* Ship's accommodations is extremely wide. On the high side a couple in first class may have a suite with two bedrooms and baths and a sitting room for $2,930 one way on the Atlantic. On the low side, an individual in tourist class may pay as little as $210 one way. The typical first-class and cabin-class cabins compare favorably with the rooms of a fine hotel in a large city. They are very well furnished and beautifully appointed. All the first-class accommodations have baths with fresh and salt water. Most of the cabin-class rooms have baths or showers, but some are interconnecting facilities shared by two accommodations. There are many single rooms in cabin class, but if the ship were crowded, a single passenger buying his ticket late might be asked to share his accommodation. The tourist-class rooms have the least space per passenger. Some have four berths and the passengers are likely to be sharing staterooms. Most all tourist cabins have at least two berths, so that on a crowded ship the single passenger is pretty certain to be sharing his accommodation. Tourist rooms have lavatories, but baths, showers, and toilets are public in most cases.

Inside the liner, passageways were jammed with passengers, visitors, ship's stewards, bedroom maids, and others of the crew who work in the sleeping quarters. Stewards carrying three, four, or five heavy suitcases pressed through the crowds to deliver the bags to the cabins. The public office of the ship's Purser was extremely busy as passengers came to ask questions about traveling on the liner. More knowledgeable travelers immediately took an elevator down to the ship's restaurants to see the managers and select their dining-table seating arrangements. Some of the passengers and their visitors walked around the ship sightseeing. The *Elizabeth* is one of the wonders of the world's oceans, and the visitors in particular wanted a look at her.

If any one thing impressed them it was the fabulous woodwork built into the liner in the 1930's when both the wood and the craftsmen could be afforded by the makers of ships. The woods of the *Queen* Ships came from all over the earth. In the *Elizabeth*'s first-class dining room, the sightseers found paneled walls covered with London plane-tree burr, bleached and finished to a light coffee-and-milk color selected as a delicate background for ladies' evening gowns. The huge main lounge is paneled with Canadian maple cluster finished with elm burr, and the main smoking room, another immense salon, is paneled with the wood of a single chestnut tree from the Isle of Wight. All external decks are planked with Burma teak.

Some of the sightseers were interested in the art of the *Queen Elizabeth* which was commissioned during the late 1930's with many of England's leading artists and craftsmen. They provided sculpture, paintings, tapestries, decorative glass, photography, and other art forms. One of the outstanding works is above a landing of the main first-class stairs. It is a

large marquetry panel depicting Chaucer's Canterbury pilgrims, designed by the artist George Ramon and made by a
British craftsman, J. Dunn. Before Ramon's idea was accepted, artists were asked to submit their thoughts for a panel
that would represent something typically British, and one
man suggested a simple, flat gray panel picturing fog. Ramon's
pilgrims required the use of sixty-six different kinds of wood
from England, Ireland, Canada, Australia, India, and several
other countries in North and South America, the West
Indies, and Scandinavia. The woods include those with common names, like sycamore, maple, and pine, and with uncommon names, like zebrano, colo bolo, laburnum, and
primavera. The panel was originally mounted in the main
lounge, but was moved to the landing and replaced by a painting of Queen Elizabeth, now the Queen Mother.

Everything about the liner is on a grand and elegant scale
that takes the beholder back several decades. An English
writer who had seen her just prior to Voyage 424 was left with
such an impression. "The thing is an institution," wrote Eric
Newby in the *London Observer,* "Not only to the British but
to multitudes of Americans who travel in her for a foretaste of
what they believe to be the British way of life, perhaps the
only part of their visit to Britain that really lives up to the
expectations." Newby described the passengers' encounter
with the *Elizabeth* as comparable to what they might have
found in "some pre-war Grand Hotel, or . . . a country house
designed by Lord Beaverbrook . . ." And he continued: "One
half expects to meet Garbo, wearing a turban, marching up one
of the innumerable grand staircases for an assignation with
John Barrymore to the strains of music played by Marcel Torrent and the Palm Court Orchestra in the Main Lounge."

The passengers arriving for Voyage 424 were men and
women from all walks of life. They included the presidents
and chairmen of the boards of great companies, college profes-

sors and scientists, royalty from Britain and India, the pub-
lisher of a London newspaper, actors and actresses, doctors and
salesmen, writers and diplomats, and hundreds of others.

The most famous man to sail that day was without doubt
David Dubinsky, who had just retired after many years as
leader of the famous International Ladies Garment Workers
Union. He and his wife came aboard, followed by newspaper
reporters and photographers. Later the journalists inter-
viewed and photographed a Broadway star, Polly James, who
had just finished an engagement in the play *Half a Sixpence,*
and was now on her way to a new role in a London theater.

The departure or arrival of celebrities on a *Queen* Ship is
invariably worth a story and photograph. At times they require major press conferences which have to be arranged and
held in a hurry by Cunard officials. One of the largest and
most nerve-racking conferences came when the evangelist
Billy Graham sailed for Europe aboard the *Queen Mary.* Everything was ready for him to meet the press in the liner's
exclusive restaurant, the Verandah Grill. But as he was boarding the ship, a Cunard information officer noted that the Reverend Graham's seat had been placed at a most inappropriate
spot in front of a famous mural painted along the restaurant's
forward wall by Doris Zinkeisen. The chair had been located
so that every photograph of the evangelist would include a
nude Negro dancer on the mural a few feet away. In a matter
of minutes, the entire arrangement had to be turned around
so that the celebrity would have his back to some drapes
drawn across the windows on the after wall. The dark drapes
with golden stars were much appreciated as a background by
the Reverend Graham.

No celebrity on a *Queen* Ship has come up with a picture
for the press that equaled the one provided by a fifty-four-year-
old British businessman, Edgar Foster. With a first-class ticket
he boarded the *Queen Elizabeth* one sailing day and immedi-

ately went to the Sun Deck where he stripped down to swimming trunks worn under his suit. Foster then climbed atop an
outside railing and did a beautiful swan dive some eighty feet
into the water. When he returned, dripping wet, to the *Elizabeth*'s gangway, the ship's officials were at a loss as to how to
admonish a favored first-class customer. The next day the New
York *Daily News* carried a large photograph of Foster sailing
down the liner's side. It had been taken by *"Daily News
Fotog"* George Torrie, who just happened to be located, cam-
era in hand, on the Sun Deck near Foster as he took the
dive.

By 11 a.m. many of the passengers for Voyage 424 were in
their cabins holding farewell parties with champagne. Saying
good-bye on a big liner is seldom a sad affair, especially for
American passengers headed for holidays in Europe. Indeed,
the visitors sometimes have such a good time at the farewell
gatherings that they fail to hear the warning gongs announc-
ing that it is time to go ashore. Occasionally such merry-
making visitors have to be taken off the liner down the
Hudson by a tugboat. One woman visitor grew sleepy at a bon-
voyage party in the 1950's and stepped into an adjoining cabin
for a nap. When she woke up, the *Queen Elizabeth* was far out
at sea. The woman was forced to go all the way to Southampton while back at home in Massachusetts her chagrined
husband mailed the Cunard company a full round-trip fare.

By 11:30 a.m. stewards were walking through the passenger quarters and public rooms ringing the all-ashore gongs.
Voyage 424 was about to begin, and visitors had to leave. Once
ashore, many went to the far end of the Cunard pier where
they could watch the big vessel steam away down the Hudson.

In the ship's wheelhouse, the *Elizabeth*'s officers and crew
were at their stations for the undocking. Commodore Marr
was there wearing his bridge coat and leather gloves. On the
flying bridge the weather was wet and miserable with winds

gusting up to 30 or 35 miles per hour. Occasionally the ship's superstructure was drenched by exceptionally heavy showers. New York's tall buildings were not even visible at times. It was truly a bad day.

Two pilots were with Commodore Marr. One was Captain Thomas Port of the Sandy Hook Pilots Association who had been assigned to take the *Queen Elizabeth* out to sea. The other was Captain Grover A. Sanschagrin, the Reynolds pilot who would soon be working by walkie-talkie radio with two Moran tugboats to undock the *Queen Elizabeth*.

While they waited for the exact time of embarkation, the Commodore and the pilots chatted about routine matters. Commodore Marr told of how lovely were the gardens at the home he had visited in Greenwich. "The crocuses are just coming out," he said. "The rain will help them along I'm sure."

In a more serious vein, the men talked about the storm still raging on the North Atlantic. "Did you read in the papers this morning about the *Michelangelo?*" asked the Commodore. "I saw that two people were killed on board."

"I thought it was three," said Captain Port.

"There are also reports that five men were swept off a banana boat," said the Commodore. "It must be the storm that passed Bermuda just as we were leaving there the other day."

That morning the early reports of damage and death at sea were confused. It turned out later that the bridge and bow of the *Michelangelo* were heavily damaged by a giant wave, and five persons were killed and eleven injured. The same storm swept five men off the refrigerated cargo ship *Chuscal,* and the U.S. Coast Guard spent nearly two days trying, without success, to find survivors.

At 11:50 a.m., Commodore Marr unceremoniously ordered his officers to set sail for Cherbourg and Southampton.

It was low slack water with the tide about to start flooding. This would allow the ship to stem the tide as she steamed down the river and out of the harbor. The Commodore had just been informed that all passengers were aboard, all visitors were ashore, and the gangways were removed and wheeled back into the pier.

The ship's officers on the bridge relayed a series of orders through their walkie-talkies to fellow officers on the *Elizabeth's* bow and stern to release the lines making the ship fast to Pier 92. As the heavy lines were dropped off the pier one at a time by dockworkers they were pulled up onto the liner's deck by the electrically driven capstans.

"Let us know when all the propellers are clear," called out Commodore Marr as the lines were hauled in. With the ship about to back into the Hudson River, he wanted to make certain that no ropes were hanging down over the vessel's stern to tangle with the propellers as the blades began to turn.

"All clear aft," called out Junior First Officer Finlay when he had learned by radio that the after ropes were up and out of the way.

The next order came from Captain Sanschagrin in a remarkably low voice. "Full astern two port," he said.

The order was repeated in louder voices by the quartermasters and the two telegraphs at the port side of the wheelhouse were pulled back to the "Full Astern" position which signaled for the start of the two port engines at 100 revolutions per minute. Captain Sanschagrin's second order followed immediately: "Slow astern two starboard." The two starboard propellers were started in reverse at 60 revolutions per minute.

The liner began backing out of her slip, but with the port turning faster than the starboard propellers, the stern was forced slightly away from the pier. The movement astern, however, was so slow that many of the passengers and their friends on the pier didn't realize immediately that the liner was underway.

It took a full ten minutes for the *Queen Elizabeth* to back out into the river, completely clear of the pier. Meanwhile, Captain Sanschagrin continued his relaxed, quiet orders, both to the liner's crew and his tugboat captains commanding the *Carol* and *Moira Moran* down below. As the *Elizabeth* slid out into the Hudson, the *Moira* began pushing hard on her starboard quarter, while the *Carol* pressed firmly against her starboard bow. The *Carol*'s role was that of a pivot on which to swing the liner stern first up the river. The *Moira* provided some of the power to swing the 83,000-ton liner like the hand of a giant clock. Additional force came from the *Elizabeth*'s own power. As she was clearing the pier, Captain Sanschagrin called for "Full Astern" on both starboard engines and for the two port engines to be stopped. This helped to revolve the ship in coordination with the tugs.

But it was a tough job because the ebbing tide was producing a down-river current. The *Elizabeth* was not only damming up part of the current, but trying to push it back up the Hudson as her stern was forced northward. When she was far enough out into the stream so that her bow would clear the Italian Line pier, Captain Sanschagrin stopped fighting the tide and let it work for him. He ordered the *Carol* to release the liner's bow, but he kept the *Moira* pushing hard on the stern. Thus the pivotal point suddenly shifted from stem to stern, and the tide was allowed to sweep the *Elizabeth*'s bow around and down the river. The immense liner was on her way.

Actually the undocking was a short and simple operation compared to the docking. In a few minutes, Captain Sanschagrin's work was done; he shook hands with Commodore Marr, bid him good-bye, and went down through the ship and out of a shell door where he boarded a waiting tug. The *Carol* and *Moira* immediately departed for other jobs, and the *Queen Elizabeth* proceeded under her own power. Captain Port, the Sandy Hook pilot, was now giving the orders that determined the course from the Hudson River to the open sea.

"Steer one-nine-six," said the pilot standing at a window in the front of the wheelhouse. Chief Quartermaster Bell, repeating the compass heading, turned the liner's wheel to bring her to that course, just slightly to the southwest.

Rain was beating against the wheelhouse windows, and the speed of the wind striking the ship was increasing as she sailed slowly toward the Upper Bay. The city lay under a ceiling of heavy gray mist and smog that hid the top of the Empire State Building. To the south the buildings in the famous skyline were intermittently visible but even then they were difficult to discern.

From the bridge, the pilot and officers could look straight out at the forward mast where several deck hands on rope ladders high above the main deck were hard at work tying down the rigging which had been used for handling cargo during the turnaround. More men were working in the rain on the deck below. All were wet and cold, and they hurried to secure the cargo hatches and the rigging that went with them. The farther the *Elizabeth* moved out into the Upper Bay, the rougher it became for these seamen.

One of the busiest of the ship's crew right now was Harold Bretherton, a rotund Englishman who is the *Queen Elizabeth*'s Chief Master at Arms—in other words, her police and fire chiefs combined. With several of his fourteen masters at arms he was systematically searching the *Elizabeth*'s maze of cubicles, corners, and alleyways for stowaways who are still a problem even in modern ships. The *Queen*'s stowaway search is a big task because there are so many hiding places, and it has to be done fast in order to return any offenders by tugboat before the liner is too far out of the harbor.

Bretherton and his men found no stowaways on Voyage 424, but when the ship was out to sea on the next sailing from New York they were to find an unticketed Chicago traveler with a gun and 120 rounds of ammunition. This bad customer claimed he was heading for Poland to "liberate" his girl friend. He was locked in a guarded detention room for a round trip on the *Elizabeth* to Southampton and back to New York where he was delivered to the police.

"We have one or two stowaways a season," says Bretherton. "And of course there could be some we don't find who get away with it. It gets harder and harder to recognize a stowaway. Used to be that everyone on board was well dressed, but today you're likely to find even some of the best-paying first-class passengers dressed like beatniks. Back in the time when all passengers dressed well, the stowaway usually stood out in the crowd because his poor clothes were conspicuous. But now they can come aboard as visitors and mingle with the passengers as the ship undocks and even gets way out to sea. Who can tell a stowaway from a proper paying beatnik? It's hard. But it's at night that we're likely to find them. They have a problem locating a place to sleep. They'll be caught hanging around in the public rooms hoping to sleep on a lounge. Food isn't the problem you might expect because they'll live on candy bars and crackers that can be bought in the shops aboard. Or they can go sit in a deck chair and be served tea and crackers. Still we don't find many such fellows."

One of the most memorable stowaways to take the *Queen Elizabeth* was fifteen-year-old Ronald Mooney of Sea Cliff, Long Island. Ronald later told reporters, "The summer was getting sort of dull, and I thought of this [stowing away]." With only $30 in his pocket, he packed a rucksack with a few of his things and rode a train to New York. Looking around the docks, he picked the biggest ship in sight—the *Queen Elizabeth*—and went aboard as a visitor. The masters at arms failed to recognize Ronald's illegal status during the stowaway search going down the harbor. As the vast ship stood out to sea, Ronald roamed her passageways, decks, and public rooms as he pleased. That night at sea the boy decided he should let the folks at home know of his venture, so he nonchalantly went up to the radio room and sent them a wireless, which read: "Don't worry. Off to England! Back for school. Love, Ron." His parents in Sea Cliff immediately called Cunard officials who in turn radioed the *Elizabeth* to look for Ronald. He was soon found and placed in a stowaways' room (for the nondangerous variety) across the passageway from Bretherton's quarters. The boy didn't visit England, though the ship's crew allowed him to touch one foot ashore from the Southampton gangway—just so he could tell his friends back home he had been in Europe. On his return to New York, Ronald was met by the FBI and his parents who had already paid his round-trip fare. The FBI warned him that his offense—should he try it again—could get him a year in jail, or $1,000 fine, or both. The parents' remarks to Ronald were never a matter of record.

As Voyage 424 began, and Bretherton conducted the stowaway search, other crew members assembled the passengers for the traditional lifesaving drill, the only one of the voyage. Loudspeakers called people to come from their cabins to the promenade deck with the life jackets that are found in all accommodations. As they lined up, the passengers were told how to use the life jackets, and were assigned to lifeboat stations. In an emergency each person would proceed to one of the *Elizabeth*'s twenty-six steel lifeboats that can be lowered by a single crewman in a few seconds. Each lifeboat carries 145 persons, which is greater than the passenger capacity of the first liner built for Cunard, the *Britannia* (1840).

The lifesaving exercise over, the passengers returned to their cabins and then many proceeded to the first of scores of parties that would be held on the *Queen Elizabeth* during Voyage 424. Undoubtedly the biggest, most crowded party was getting underway in the quarters of the ship's Purser, Fergus Pritchard. Here, in two small rooms, stood a large, closely packed group of first-class passengers invited for cocktails before their first luncheon aboard the ship. Pritchard, who has been a ship's purser with Cunard since the late 1920's, met people at the door and, in his customary way, demonstrated an amazing memory for names. Upon learning each newcomer's name, he led the person around his quarters and introduced him to everyone in the continually expanding party. Pritchard's introductions employed names and titles with precision. He acted as if he had known everyone there for years, though he was actually meeting most of the guests for the first time. As the size of the party grew, Pritchard's name-remembering feat became more and more remarkable. When finally he brought the last arrival around the room, the Purser introduced him to about thirty-five people by their names.

The room was extremely crowded and noisy, but no one cared, for it was fun to move about and meet one's fellow passengers. The people who travel on such a luxury liner can be a varied and interesting lot. At one moment in the party, for example, a New York advertising executive and his wife on their first trans-Atlantic voyage (he on business, she for pleasure) found themselves chatting with a beautiful and gracious Indian lady wearing her delightfully colored, flowing sari. She was the Marchioness of Winchester traveling to England with her brother, a doctor from Malabar Hill, Bombay, India. On the other side of the crowded quarters a young man traveling alone and obviously interested in the few young ladies present, made a misstep and suddenly found himself trapped, face-to-face in a corner with an elderly, monologic dowager from Cambridge, Massachusetts. She was on her way to Europe to spend the spring and summer. After several minutes covering several subjects, the woman interrupted herself as she glanced through a nearby porthole and noted that the *Queen Elizabeth* was going under a bridge.

"Is that the George Washington Bridge?" asked the lady.

The baffled young man didn't know if she were teasing or not. "If it is," he said with an awkward laugh, "we're going the wrong way."

Of course, it was the Verrazano-Narrows Bridge.

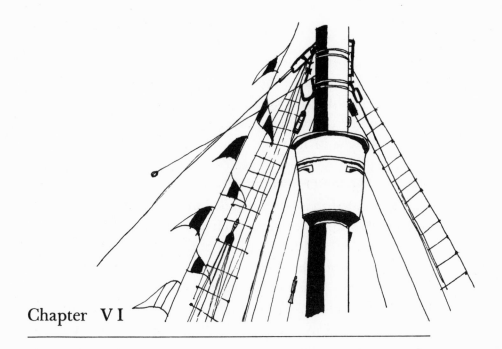

Chapter VI

Dropping the Pilot at Ambrose

As the *Queen Elizabeth* crossed New York Harbor's Upper Bay guided by the Sandy Hook pilot, Captain Thomas Port, her master, Commodore Marr, checked the *Queen*'s main radar set. A marvelous, complex piece of navigational equipment from this age of computers, it stands in contrast to the comparatively simple bridge. The 16-inch horizontal radar screen is on a waist-high console in a wooden, closet-like enclosure directly behind the liner's helm. The enclosure blocks the light from the forward windows, and allows two or three

men to stand inside to view the radar picture. While Commodore Marr watched the screen, it was scanned by a radial
line of light, like the rapidly moving hand of a clock. As it
swept around the viewing area, the line left orange-colored
images of light in its wake. Between each sweep, the images
slowly faded, but were repeatedly strengthened as the line
kept passing by. One could recognize in the orange images
what amounted to a fairly detailed outline map of New York
Harbor. In the screen's lower left quadrant was the southern
part of Manhattan Island with its dozens of piers projecting at
right angles from the shore. Higher on the same side of the
screen was the outline of Governor's Island and the shores of
Brooklyn beyond it. To the right were Ellis Island and Liberty Island, and at the top left of the screen appeared the
Narrows with a sharp straight line indicating the Verrazano-
Narrows Bridge.

From the top center a fixed straight line of light extended
down across the circular screen and ended several inches directly below the center. The line's lower tip represented on
the radar map the liner's momentary position and its longitude indicated the course the *Queen Elizabeth* would take
should she continue on her present heading. As she sailed
forward, the line automatically grew shorter to account for
her movement along the represented course. Right now the
line's bottom end placed the liner slightly southwest of the tip
of Manhattan Island, and the lay of the line showed that she
was on a course out across the Upper Bay toward Staten Island. In a few minutes, however, the pilot ordered her slightly
around to port, and as the Chief Quartermaster brought the
ship a few degrees to the left, the radar map automatically
revolved clockwise the same number of degrees. Thus the entire outline of the harbor turned. Staten Island, for instance,
swung a few degrees around to the right. But the line representing the *Elizabeth*'s course remained fixed so that now it

extended out through the Narrows—and that's where the big liner was heading.

Commodore Marr was intrigued with this radar, which at the time of Voyage 424 was comparatively new for the *Elizabeth*. It had been installed by its English manufacturer, the Marconi International Marine Company Limited. When the Commodore discovered that Captain Port had not really seen the device at work, he took the opportunity to tell him about it.

"You can step back here for a minute, Pilot, and look at the radar," said the Commodore. "It will show you where we're going practically as well as looking out the forward windows.

"This is a true-motion radar in which a computer feeds the ship's course and speed into the thing. Now the ship moves across the screen along this line which is pointing directly toward the center of the bow.

"This system is absolutely marvelous. It puts you in the position of somebody in an airplane a few thousand feet above the ship looking down over the harbor watching the *Queen Elizabeth* go down past Manhattan—but watching all the other ships moving at the same time.

"Over here we have two ships," continued the Commodore, pointing to two spots on the screen near the radar picture of Staten Island. "And here is a ferry coming out of Staten Island. And over there is a string of barges. Now let's take a look forward, Pilot, and see if we see them." They walked from the radar enclosure around to the front windows and, through rain and mist, picked out all the vessels represented on the screen.

Had such a clear radar picture been available in 1959, the *Queen Elizabeth* undoubtedly would have avoided the only collision in her history of travel through busy New York Harbor. At that time, she was creeping along in a dense fog

over Ambrose Channel off Coney Island. Suddenly through
the murk appeared a freighter, the *American Hunter,* and,
before the crews of either vessel could prevent it, her prow
plowed into the *Elizabeth*'s bow. The liner turned back to
survey the damage, which turned out to be minor: two small
holes in the hull near the starboard anchor. That is, the holes
were small for the size of the liner; it still took ten tons of
concrete to plug them up temporarily so she could proceed to
England for permanent repairs. But such a collision could
hardly happen with the latest radar. The *American Hunter*
would have been clearly represented on the screen and
avoided long before she came close to the big liner. Not that
the *Elizabeth* had no radar in 1959; she did, but the representa-
tion of what lay ahead left a lot to be desired in a heavy fog.

"From the point of view of a ship's master," says Commodore Marr about the latest equipment, "it's difficult to express what a tremendous advantage this kind of radar is to our
safety at sea, or coming into a harbor during bad weather, at
night, or in the fog. It provides us with a magnificent living
map with the *Queen Elizabeth* sailing across it, at the same
time showing us every other vessel within the radar's range.

"Speaking of the range, we can turn a switch and change
it, so that the radar screen can encompass a fairly small circle
around the *Queen Elizabeth,* or by continuing to turn the
switch, make the circle progressively larger. For the shortest
range the set presents us with an area whose radius is only

This drawing illustrates what the circular screen of the Elizabeth's
*main radar set would show if the liner were approaching the scene
depicted above. The line down the screen to the center of the concentric circles represents the ship's present course. The location of
the vessel itself would be at the bottom end of the line. The space
between each ring represents two miles. The range of the screen
would be 12 miles on this particular setting, though it can be instantly adjusted to encompass as much as 48 miles.*

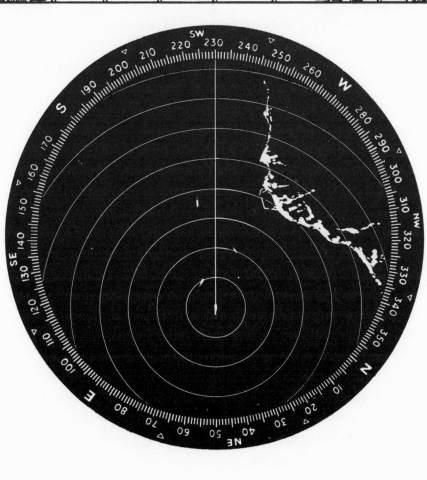

three quarters of a mile. But then we can extend the range to eight different radii. A snap of the switch and the picture takes in an area with a mile and a half radius around the ship. A couple more and it reaches out twelve miles, then eighteen, twenty-four, and finally, when we're far out on the ocean, she can give us a look at a circular expanse of sea forty-eight miles all around."

To the left of the *Elizabeth*'s main radar console is a smaller one containing a comparatively primitive, though entirely adequate, radar set. Its screen is less than half the size of the large new set, and it produces a radar map somewhat more difficult to comprehend. The small set is a stand-by radar in case the large one fails.

Satisfied that both were in good working order, Commodore Marr joined Captain Port at the fore of the wheelhouse. The ship by now had passed under the Verrazano Bridge and was heading for the Ambrose Channel.

"Full ahead," called the harbor pilot, and the ship's telegraphs were pushed forward requesting the top maneuvering revolutions of 100 per minute.

"We've had complaints of wash damage from around Brooklyn," said the Sandy Hook pilot, "so I reduced her speed through the Narrows."

The remark reminded Commodore Marr of an unusual maritime problem that he once encountered as master of a Cunard liner running between England and Montreal. "We had to keep the farmers' cows in mind on the St. Lawrence. They'd come along the shore to graze, and if we didn't hold down our speed, the wash would knock them over. The home office would then hear from the outraged farmers."

While the Commodore was telling his anecdote, the *Queen Elizabeth*'s second in command, Staff Captain F. J. Storey, reported to the bridge. The Staff Captain of a Cunard liner is the Captain's deputy, responsible for the proper administration of all departments on board. This includes the general discipline, efficiency, and coordination of the ship's crew, the cleanliness of the vessel, the storing of the ship, and everything or anything related to the safety, comfort, and general well-being of the passengers. In addition the Staff Captain is expected to perform whatever navigating duties the Captain may require of him.

Captain Storey, who has been going to sea since 1928, waited politely for the Commodore to finish his tale from the St. Lawrence River, and then reported that all was well below. "Would you like to have lunch now?" he asked the Commodore. "I am free to remain here."

"But have you had your lunch, Captain?" asked the ship's master.

"Not as yet."

"I am not particularly hungry," said the Commodore, "so I will stay here until we leave off the pilot. Please, go ahead and have your lunch."

Meanwhile the pilot was ordering headings that determined the course from the Narrows out into the Ambrose Channel. "Steer one-one-seven," he commanded as the liner came into the last long stretch of channel leading to Ambrose Lightship and the open sea.

Slowly the huge *Queen Elizabeth* steamed out between Sandy Hook and Rockaway Point, the two promontories forming the wide mouth to the harbor's Lower Bay. The vessel was leaving the protection of the land, and her prow struck the first of the rough, open sea. Her rigging, hatches, and everything else on the open decks had been secured. All but two crewmen had left the main deck below the bridge, and they worked hard and fast to finish their jobs.

The stiff, gusty wind, now striking the vessel from off the ocean, cut through her rigging and hurled rain and spray over the liner's white superstructure, rattling the bridge windows

and the sliding doors at the side of the wheelhouse. The gale
set up a deep howl, modulated by the strong gusts, that would
be heard on the bridge unceasingly for the next several
days.

Only a few of more than a dozen officers and men present
during the undocking were still in the wheelhouse. Commodore Marr had relieved all but those on the ship's regular
noon-to-4-o'clock watch. This included the Senior First
Officer, J. A. B. Munro, the Senior Third, R. Dootson, two
quartermasters, and two able seamen as bridge boys. Munro
walked back and forth at the front of the wheelhouse, detour-
ing around Commodore Marr and the pilot. Dootson was in
one of two rooms aft of the wheelhouse where he worked with
the ship's charts that would be used once the *Elizabeth*
dropped the pilot by Ambrose Lightship and stood out to sea.
One of the quartermasters was taking a spell at the wheel,
steering the ship while the other directed the bridge boys on a
round of cleaning that continues without let-up during a voyage.

It was approaching 2 o'clock when Commodore Marr
called out the command: "Slow ahead all!" The ship's telegraphs were pulled back to the "Slow Ahead" position, and
her four propellers reduced to 60 revolutions per minute.
Commodore Marr and Captain Port had just spotted the
Sandy Hook Association's pilot launch coming toward the
Elizabeth to pick up the pilot and carry him a few miles back
to the 215-foot pilot station boat now hidden by the bad
weather.

"How long will you be out here?" Commodore Marr
asked Captain Port who was preparing to leave the bridge.

"I expect it will be about midnight," said the pilot. He
would wait in turn with fellow pilots for his next assignment,
probably on an inbound cargo ship or oil tanker. Captain Port
shook hands with the Commodore, bid everyone good-bye,

and left by the rear door. The Commodore stepped around to a wheelhouse window where he could watch the pilot launch, which looked like a toy boat as she closed in on the *Elizabeth*. The actions of the small vessel revealed that this, indeed, was a rough day on the ocean, for the launch seemed to be climbing hills and coasting into valleys as she sailed up over the waves and down across the troughs.

She moved in on the liner's towering starboard side where there was the most protection from the wind and bad weather. The launch paralleled the *Elizabeth* and then slid in toward the black, wet hull to a point where Captain Port was standing in a shell door on "R" deck. When she was in place, the pilot launch was riding with her bow just under the door. A cold, wet deck hand on the launch was ready to help the pilot down a rope ladder which was quickly lowered from the liner. Captain Port stepped out of the ship's door and descended to the launch which was bobbing and swaying on the ocean as it sailed along with the huge ship. It is crucial to keep the small vessel aligned with the big one under these rough conditions. Should the two vessels suddenly pull apart, a valuable man could be dropped into the ice-cold sea, and fishing him out might be extremely difficult. But Captain Port, who had made the short, treacherous trip hundreds of times before, nimbly climbed down the swaying ladder, ten or twelve feet long, and in a moment, jumped from the last rung to the deck of the launch. At that second, a wave bashed over the small boat's bow and the Sandy Hook pilot, complete with business suit and fedora, received a thorough dousing.

Commodore Marr saw the pilot get wet. With the collar of his heavy bridge coat pulled up around his neck and his white-topped hat pulled on tightly, the liner's Master was watching from high on the wing of the stormy bridge, where he had gone to make sure that Captain Port transferred safely from the *Elizabeth* to the launch. Munro, the officer of the watch, had also come outside and was looking down at the launch. Captain Port, suspecting that he was being watched, looked up to the flying bridge and waved. He then brushed the sea water from his coat, took off his felt hat, gave it a shake, and dashed for the cabin of the pilot launch as it rapidly pulled away from the liner.

Actually, he and his fellow pilots transfer from ships to the pilot launch in worse weather than this. Sometimes, for instance, both the launch and the bigger vessel are covered with thick coatings of rime. Should conditions at the Ambrose Lightship be too bad for a safe transfer, the pilot may have a long steamship ride before he gets home again. This has only happened to a very few pilots.

Commodore Marr tells of how he took one of England's most famous pilots, Captain Jack Holt, on a Christmas holiday tour one year. "He piloted the *Queen Mary* out of Southampton with a special cruise conducted by the *News of the World*. Once the *Mary* was outside of Southampton water, it was impossible for Jack to leave, so he went on down to Las Palmas for the six-day cruise. We had some fun with Jack by threatening to put him to work as cruise director."

Certain that Captain Port was safely off the *Queen Elizabeth,* Commodore Marr turned and momentarily looked out over the bow at the rough sea ahead. Wind and salt water mixed with rain were hitting him in the face. Munro started for the wheelhouse, but stopped abruptly to listen to the Commodore, who suddenly began reciting a poem.

> *"He is no fair weather sailor,*
>   *It has long been his boast,*
>   *That the ocean deeps are far safer*
>   *Than the wild New England coast."*

While he was still reciting the last line, the Commodore turned and walked briskly back into the wheelhouse followed by a smiling Munro. The liner's Master frequently picks such a dramatic moment to recite poetry, and the officer of the watch was not surprised.

"What is that from?" asked Munro as the two men entered the wheelhouse.

"I really don't know," said Commodore Marr. "It's something my mother used to recite to me when I was young and only thinking about going to sea."

Inside, the Commodore immediately called out a loud, sharp command: "Ring her away! Tell the engine room one-seven-zero revolutions!"

The telegraphs were briefly pulled back to the stop position and then shoved forward all the way. The procedure informed the liner's engineers that the 100-revolution maximum of maneuvering revs no longer applied. They were to work up the engines to a new maximum of 170 revolutions—a number that was promptly telephoned from the bridge down to the engine rooms. The new revs, for running at sea, would produce about 28 knots, depending on the wind and sea. This maximum chosen by the Commodore was just four revolutions short of the liner's cruising maximum: 174.

The ring-away order, issued at 2 p.m., Eastern Standard Time, marked the official departure time from the Port of New York on Voyage 424. The liner had undocked promptly and then made such good time in the harbor that she was a half hour ahead of schedule. Commodore Marr was pleased because the thirty minutes gained allowed for unexpected delays which might occur in the next four days. It might also provide the opportunity to save fuel by using fewer engine revolutions toward the end of the voyage.

"By holding the engines back as little as six revolutions per minute," explains the Commodore, "it is entirely possible to save from a hundred to a hundred and fifty tons of fuel in crossing the Atlantic. At twenty-four dollars per ton, or so, this turns out to be a worthwhile saving, you see."

A *Queen* Ship does not immediately come up to full speed at a command from her master. She takes four hours. First, because a ship of 83,000 tons has tremendous inertia, she simply requires time to get going. On the other hand, she cannot be stopped in a hurry. No one knows how far the *Elizabeth* would coast should all her power be suddenly removed at top speed, but educated estimates put it at almost ten miles. Even a "crash stop,"—when the propellers are quickly reversed—would take an estimated five miles. These emergency stops have never been tested, however, for they would subject the engines to the possibility of extremely serious damage.

The second reason that it takes four hours to move up to her higher speeds is that the *Queen Elizabeth* uses superheated steam. On maneuvering revs her sixteen turbines draw steam directly from her twelve boilers, but as revolutions are increased over 100 per minute, the steam is superheated. It is drawn from the boilers as before, but then it is conducted back into special tubes that pass through the seven oil fires in each boiler. The steam is thus reheated, raising both its temperature and pressure to offer extra driving power for the ship's turbines. The engines, however, cannot be suddenly introduced to superheated steam without risking serious damage to the comparatively delicate turbine blades. When they are finally whirling full speed with superheated steam, the blades are greatly expanded by the tremendous heat. But should the blades, when cool and contracted, be suddenly exposed to the full measure of superheated steam they would be forced to expand so fast that the metal might be ruined. Nor can the superheated steam be stopped suddenly, for drastic contraction of the metal could also damage the turbine blades. Therefore the *Queen Elizabeth* must speed up gradually over the four-hour period and slow down in the same amount of time, except in an emergency serious enough to risk damaging the turbines.

In the four hours after Commodore Marr rang her away, the engines' speed would be steadily but slowly increased from 100 to 170. At the end of the first hour the revolutions would be passing 140. The second would take them by 152, the third past 165, and by the fourth hour they would have reached 170.

Like a violin or even the human chest cavity, a great ship like the *Elizabeth* has certain resonant frequencies. The ranges 140 to 145 and 150 to 162 revolutions are the *Elizabeth*'s "critical revolutions" that set up vibrations which are in resonance with the ship's structure. Should she vibrate for long at these frequencies, it could build upon itself until the vessel shook violently enough to damage herself—to say nothing about the psychological effect on passengers. Her Master and engineers, therefore, avoid speed settings that would require the ship's engines to run within the critical revolutions.

After Commodore Marr had rung her away, he decided, in consultation with the officers of the watch, on an initial compass heading. It would stand the ship on a course parallel to Long Island and out toward Nantucket Island. With this, the long day-and-night routine of taking the *Queen Elizabeth* across the North Atlantic on Voyage 424 had begun.

"I believe I will go down for a bite of lunch," said the Commodore to his officer, and walked out of the wheelhouse.

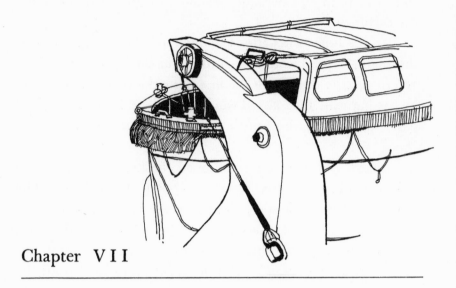

Chapter VII

The First Afternoon

It was nearly 3 o'clock when Commodore Marr returned to the navigation bridge after a light lunch in his quarters. He went forward in the wheelhouse and spoke with Munro as they both looked through the rain-spotted windows at the ocean ahead. The sea was growing increasingly rough as the slowly accelerating liner moved east from Ambrose.

"I'd say force six, gusting force seven, Munro," said the Commodore, studying the surface of the sea ahead, and Munro agreed. To these mariners, force six and seven is the measure of a pretty rough sea, as interpreted by the "Beaufort scale" of wind force. The scale classifies the visual appearance of the sea as an indication of wind speed and storm conditions. At force zero it says: "Sea like a mirror," indicating the wind is under one knot. At force three, a "gentle breeze," seven to ten knots, is revealed by a sea described as: "Small wavelets. Crests begin to break. Foam of glassy appearance. Perhaps scattered white horses." (White horses are waves with foamy crests.) Force seven, mentioned by the Commodore, reads: "Sea heaps up, and white foam from breaking waves begins to be blown in streaks along the direction of the wind." This indicates "near gale" winds of 28-33 knots producing waves over 13 feet high.

"The wind hitting the *Michelangelo* when she was damaged yesterday," said Commodore Marr, "was reported at sixty-five knots. Do you realize what that means?"

"Yes, sir," said Munro, shaking his head.

"The wave that did the damage and killed the people on the *Michelangelo*," added the Commodore, "was reported to be over thirty feet high. You know, Munro, if we get waves thirty feet high we had better watch out even in a ship this size."

The Commodore soon walked back through the wheelhouse to the weather chart room on the port side where he began studying a weather map for the Atlantic. It was spread out on a drafting table having been prepared earlier by one of the ship's officers. Isobars developed from meteorological data radioed that morning from Washington, D.C., were superimposed upon an outline map of the ocean. The Atlantic's eastern half was almost completely filled by a large concentric pattern of isobars representing the low-pressure pattern creating the storm currently causing so much trouble for shipping.

"This little storm which didn't look too bad when it

passed Bermuda Sunday evening," said the Commodore, partly talking to himself and partly to the ship's Senior Third Officer, R. Dootson, "has turned into a real wrecker, a real monster which has caused a great deal of havoc. You very seldom have a storm of that dimension. The weather from that storm stretches from the coast of Spain to the coast of Newfoundland, and from the coast of Iceland down south of the Azores. At Ponta Delgada they are having gale force westerly winds. In Iceland they are having gale force easterlies."

While the big storm amazed even this master mariner, he soon became most concerned with a storm of comparatively minor proportions centered just off Nantucket. This was the low-pressure system causing the rain encountered all the way out of New York. It was moving northeastward, and the Commodore suspected it would eventually bump into the devastating but slow-moving weather system west of Europe.

After studying the chart he decided to take the *Queen Elizabeth* along the southern edge of the nearby low-pressure system. He felt he could do so by proceeding to the Nantucket Shoals Lightship and then generally eastward to the beginning of a southern steamship lane known as Track "B." At the moment this course headed for the storm's center, but the ship would not arrive there for twelve hours or so, and by then the system's northeastward migration would leave the liner on the southern side of the low-pressure area. Thus the *Elizabeth* would steam along with the wind which would be blowing west to east. In low-pressure areas on the North Atlantic the air flows counterclockwise around the center (the reverse being true of high-pressure systems).

"When the wind comes from the ship's stern," explains the Commodore, "that's pennies from heaven. The wind may be moving at a good speed across the sea, but the *Queen Elizabeth* can move right along with it. On the deck then it is a calm day. The passengers can go outside and enjoy themselves, not even realizing that they're sailing across a very windy stretch of the ocean.

"When the wind is on the bow, it's a very different matter. As we work up to our speed, some twenty-eight knots, with a windspeed of twenty-five knots coming at us from over the ocean—that's twenty-eight plus twenty-five, which gives you fifty-three knots. That's force ten, which on the Beaufort scale is listed as a storm. And standing on the deck of the *Queen Elizabeth* would be next to impossible."

Commodore Marr is known to his officers as truly a master navigator. He is especially expert at dealing with the Atlantic's complex weather to give his passengers the smoothest and safest possible journey. When he can, he likes to do the kind of "pressure pattern navigating" he was considering here on Voyage 424. It is employed extensively in modern aircraft navigation, where jets have more chance of success with the method than ships. Fast-flying planes can travel around large weather patterns before the patterns have a chance to change much. Ships moving at about a tenth the speed of planes can also make good use of such navigation, if the masters are expert meteorologists as well as good sailors. Not only must the sea captain navigate in anticipation of immediate weather changes, like the jet pilot, but in addition he must think in terms of several days ahead. Voyage 424 is a case in point. It put Commodore Marr's commendable skills to a severe test, for the usual Atlantic weather patterns had been turned upside down.

"The Azores' high and the Icelandic low generally dominate the weather in the Atlantic," explained the *Elizabeth*'s Master. "On an easterly crossing we then sail across the north side of the Azores' high moving along with the westerlies. Coming out of Cherbourg, steaming to America, we tend to take advantage of the southern side of the high in order to sail with the easterly winds."

On April 13 the Azores' high had been forced far to the south by the vast low-pressure system west of Europe, and therefore the usual Atlantic weather was reversed. The second low near Nantucket further complicated the already unusual situation.

One more unhappy thought about Atlantic weather was running through Commodore Marr's mind as he set sail on Voyage 424: The Atlantic's prevailing weather patterns move from west to east usually at a speed not far different from the *Elizabeth*'s 28 knots. Thus bad weather at the beginning of an easterly voyage may accompany the ship for thousands of miles. Sailing from Europe, however, the westbound ship passes by or through the eastbound weather so a storm, though bad, is not likely to last too long.

When Commodore Marr had determined his liner's overall course, which he hoped would take the *Elizabeth* below the Nantucket storm, he gave his officers the necessary compass headings and left the bridge. He went directly to his quarters, completed some paperwork, and took a short nap, knowing it might be a long way to bedtime. Moreover, the weather being what it was, he could hardly expect an uninterrupted night's rest. While he napped, the officers of the watch on the bridge directly above the Commodore's quarters carried out his navigational orders.

The *Queen Elizabeth*'s navigators work with many navigational aids. On the one hand they use methods and equipment developed and passed down from ages of men crossing the oceans. They also turn to devices that are practically on the frontier of navigational technology.

At the *Queen Elizabeth*'s helm her quartermaster, that gray April afternoon, was guided by a gyroscopic compass, which is central to all directional equipment on the ship. With no more than this compass, a dependable timepiece, and accurate charts, her officers can take the liner across the entire

Atlantic by "DR" (dead reckoning). With DR they follow one carefully chosen compass heading after another, each for a specific length of time, until they have covered their planned course. How long they spend on each heading is determined by the vessel's speed calculated from the propeller revolutions minus "slip." This final factor, figured out jointly by the bridge and the engineering department, accounts for the waste motion of the propellers as they force the ship forward. It depends on the head-on resistance the vessel encounters from the sea and wind. DR is an ancient procedure, yet the *Queen Elizabeth*'s officers have at times sailed her across the ocean using it as their only method of navigation. Foggy, cloudy weather then prevented the taking of navigational fixes from the stars or sun, and atmospheric conditions reduced the dependability of radio aids to navigation.

Most of the time, however, the compass is just the core of a system containing several electrical-mechanical aids that make the navigator's job more sophisticated and precise than ever before.

The most sophisticated device of the lot is the "Decca Navigator" with the trade name "Multipulse Mark 12." Made by the Decca Navigator Company Limited of London, it is a completely automatic radio position-fixing device which can instantly provide figures that allow the *Elizabeth*'s officers to spot their exact position on most of the ocean. The machine is a complicated set of radio receivers that can be tuned to special Decca transmitting stations constructed in groups of four stations 80 to 100 miles apart. One is always located roughly in the center of the other three. As their signals are received by the ship's Decca equipment, the slight differences in transmission time are used by a built-in computer to produce the data necessary for a navigator to determine the ship's position on a special Decca chart. As the *Queen Elizabeth* proceeded over the western Atlantic on Voyage 424, she used Decca stations in

the New York City area, Nova Scotia, the Gulf of St. Lawrence, and Newfoundland. In the eastern Atlantic she would
use several of the eleven groups of stations spread from
Sweden to Spain. In mid-Atlantic, however, the Decca Navigator would be turned off because the liner goes through a dead
spot that cannot be reached by transmitters on either conti-
nent.

The *Queen* Ship's officer may also use the well-known
Loran system (Long Range Radio Navigation) which, like the
Decca system, depends on measuring the time differences
taken by radio signals traveling from widely spaced transmit-
ters to the ship. The Loran is not nearly as automated as the
Multipulse 12, and therefore requires more time to pinpoint
the ship's position. On the other hand it is valuable because
Loran signals are available across the entire North Atlantic.

A third navigational tool, one associated with the mariner's trade for centuries, is the sextant. Each officer aboard the
Elizabeth owns and uses his personal sextant in clear weather
to shoot the sun and stars to fix the liner's position.

Finally, the *Elizabeth*'s navigational equipment includes
an automatic depth recorder which provides the ship's officers
with a further check upon their position. Their ocean charts,
littered with tiny numbers indicating depths from point to
point, are compared with the depth recorder's graphs to verify
the liner's position as it is fixed by other methods.

All of these devices and methods are likely to be used on
a voyage to provide the quartermaster with headings and to
check upon estimated positions as the *Elizabeth* steams across
the Atlantic.

But the ship's officers are not the only ones who continually know the liner's whereabouts. As the *Queen Elizabeth*
starts across the Atlantic, her radio operators contact the
"Automated Merchant Vessel Report System" (AMVER)
operated by the U.S. Coast Guard on Governor's Island in

New York Harbor. AMVER is given a description of the ship, her time and place of departure, proposed route, speed, destination, and estimated arrival time. The data are fed into computers that use DR procedures to predict where the ship will be at any moment. Changes in navigational plans or speed are radioed back to AMVER where the computers re-calculate the vessel's position. With the ability to process such data from hundreds of ships, AMVER offers an amazing service. Should a ship at sea need help, her master can radio AMVER and learn in a matter of minutes what ships are near him on the ocean. For instance, AMVER computers can name the ships within a 100-mile radius of the troubled vessel. The same machines can tell a troubled ship the names and radio call letters of all nearby vessels proceeding in the same general direction. Or the computers can pick out only special types of ships in the immediate area; for example, they might point out nearby vessels with doctors to help a doctorless ship with a medical emergency.

Such was the case with the freighter S.S. *Indian Trader* caught in the big Atlantic storm as the *Queen Elizabeth* began Voyage 424. Three crewmen had been badly injured and another killed aboard the 455-foot vessel about 600 miles east of New York. She sent an urgent message to AMVER whose computers revealed that only three ships with doctors lay within a 300-mile radius. They were the *Michelangelo,* already badly damaged and carrying dead and injured; the Canadian government ship *Baffin;* and the U.S. Military Sea Transport *Geiger*. The *Geiger* went to the *Indian Trader*'s assistance, but high seas prevented transfer of the most seriously hurt of the three injured men. Later that day he died.

The seas that wrought such troubles were beginning to affect the world's largest liner as it grew dark that evening of April 13, and the *Elizabeth* passed to the south of Block Island. With her propellers now at the full 170 revolutions, she

was starting to pitch as the immense hull cut through the dark
sea at 28½ knots. Certainly this was the measure of a rough
sea. The *Elizabeth* is not easily pitched by ocean waves because her long hull can usually ride astraddle several waves at
once, thereby avoiding the mountain-and-valley contours of
the sea. When the earliest *Queen* Ship, the *Mary,* was under
design, her planners felt that this first liner of over a thousand
feet might never pitch. At the time they believed that the
waves even in a bad storm did not exceed 800 feet in length,
crest to crest, and that the average was around 600. But before
the designers had finished their plans, they learned of North
Atlantic waves 50 feet high and more than a thousand feet in
length—which, of course, meant that the forthcoming liner
would not be free of pitch. However, when a *Queen* Ship does
begin pitching, it shows that she is encountering waves that
are a long way from ripples.

As night came on, the officers of the watch worked in the
wheelhouse without lights, for their eyes must be accommodated to darkness to look out from the ship to the black
ocean ahead. The only illumination came from dim little lights
on instruments and from a small, shaded lamp suspended over
a chart table on the starboard side. It illuminated a large chart
of the Atlantic on which the initial part of the liner's voyage
had been plotted in pencil. In the dark of the radar enclosure
stood a seaman assigned to watch the orange screen which now
surveyed a circular area of the stormy Atlantic, 48 miles in
diameter. Most of the screen showed mottled patterns that
consisted of tiny specks of light, each of which appeared, remained a few moments, and faded away. The specks represented the tops of the ocean's ever-changing waves which were
bouncing radar beams back to the ship. The seaman, however,
watched for more brilliant, more permanent spots that would
indicate the presence of another vessel. None were visible at
the moment, but in the last ninety minutes the seaman had

observed several vessels pass at a distance. They were bound for New York. The *Queen Elizabeth* was plying one of the ocean's busiest sea lanes.

The ship's Chief Officer, Victor Arbuckle, was now in charge of the watch. He walked back and forth along the forward wall of the wheelhouse where the wind from across the *Elizabeth*'s bow was banging and howling at the rain-drenched windows. Under these stormy conditions absolutely nothing could be seen outside, but Arbuckle, forced by years of habit, frequently glanced out the windows, as though he expected to see something.

The other officer on this four-hour stretch was the Junior Second Officer, A. C. Bennell, who remained busy with navigational details. He worked with the Decca equipment located in the little room just aft of the wheelhouse. Occasionally he checked the chart under the small light in the main room. And both he and Arbuckle frequently stepped into the radar enclosure for a look at the screen.

The two officers had little to say to one another, for they were concentrating on the duty of keeping watch over the fast-moving liner. Their work was not hurried or worried, but was carried out with a certain intensity that belied their outwardly calm and easy manner. How could these two men for a moment forget that they were in charge of an 83,000-ton behemoth driven by sixteen powerful turbines and carrying 2,456 souls through a dangerous part of the ocean? The *Elizabeth*'s bridge is strictly a place for master mariners continually on notice that they can never permit their ship to come even near a dangerous situation. A ship of 83,000 tons on the move is to be taken very seriously. She is not easily stopped or swerved.

Bennell at one point was working over the large chart in the wheelhouse as Arbuckle came by. The Junior Second pointed at Martha's Vineyard off Woods Hole, Massachusetts.

His pencil came to rest on the island's southwestern tip, called Gay Head, which would soon lie off the *Elizabeth*'s port bow.

"You know, Victor," he said, "I've seen references to Gay Head for years but didn't know anything about the place until yesterday. Do you remember reading about it in Moby Dick? Tashtego was an Indian from Gay Head. Well, I met a man in New York who goes to Martha's Vineyard in the summer. He tells me that Gay Head is still populated with Indians. This tip at the end of the island, Gay Head, isn't a town, but just a number of homes. At the very tip of the island there are cliffs overlooking the ocean, and their clay is brightly colored. They're beautiful, I understand. But my friend says that Gay Head is disappearing. The cliffs are falling into the sea at a fast rate."

"I didn't know anything about it, either," said Arbuckle. "And here we've been going by the place for years."

Chapter VIII

The First Evening

Commodore Marr visited the bridge around 6:30 p.m. to check with Arbuckle and Bennell on the ship's progress. As he arrived, the Commodore was trying to decide whether or not to go down to the first-class restaurant to eat at the Captain's table. In bad weather, and especially in fog, Commodore Marr takes his dinner in his quarters, mainly to be near the bridge, but also because he feels that psychologically it's not good to appear among his passengers when conditions are bad. They might be upset, for right or wrong, most people believe that perilous weather demands that the ship's Master be directly involved with her navigation. But tonight the Commodore decided to appear for dinner at his large circular table in the *Elizabeth*'s grand dining room several decks below. He told Arbuckle of his decision and left the bridge.

About 7:15 Commodore Marr was in his quarters, wearing a nicely pressed dark-blue dress uniform, waiting for guests who had been invited for cocktails earlier that day with small engraved cards deposited in their rooms. Soon the Captain's steward, Rowland Hill, stepped inside the curtains that veil the main door and announced the names of the first guests. In the next few minutes about fifteen people were announced by Hill, and seated in the circle of easy chairs that nearly fills the Commodore's quarters. The men wore business suits—the customary dress on the first and last nights of a voyage. All other nights in first class they wear dinner jackets and black ties. The ladies wear party dresses on the first and last nights, and evening gowns on the intervening nights. Hill took orders for cocktails and had them made and served in a few minutes. A young waiter from the main dining room passed a large tray of fancy hors d'oeuvres around the circle, and soon the conversation grew lively.

Many of the people were old hands at sailing on large passenger liners. Some had met Commodore Marr when he was the Captain of other Cunard liners, such as the *Caronia*. One man and his wife had crossed the Atlantic thirty times aboard the *Queen Elizabeth*. They were attentive as Commodore Marr spent a few minutes explaining his navigational problems. He pointed out that a bad storm engulfed the eastern Atlantic and had damaged the *Michelangelo* the day before. Everyone wanted to know if the *Elizabeth* would encounter the same storm, but the Commodore frankly admitted he could not predict that far ahead. He guessed, however, that this now famous low-pressure system would "fill" by the time his ship was in the area—which meant the storm would have largely died away.

After the cocktail party which lasted most of an hour, the entire group took an elevator down to the first-class restaurant. Commodore Marr entered the large doors at the back of the room with some of his guests and proceeded to his table located across the vast, beautifully paneled hall, 111 feet long and 111 feet wide. As he walked with long, deliberate strides, the ship's Master caught the eye of many passengers already seated for dinner. He kept bowing his head, smiling and saying "Good evening."

At his large round table which seats eight, the Commodore joined the people he had invited to dine there during the voyage. Though he hadn't met several of them, they had all met each other, for the group had assembled for lunch at the table without the Commodore. They were a varied group traveling for different reasons. On the Commodore's right was a dowager en route from her Virginia home to another of her dwellings in southern Ireland. Beside her was a television executive from New York on his way to France on business. His beautiful wife sat across the table to the Commodore's left. Both knew him from past voyages on the *Elizabeth* and the *Queen Mary,* and they addressed him as Geoffrey, which few people do. Next to the beautiful lady was a movie writer on his way from Hollywood to his London home. He had come to New York from California by jet to take the *Elizabeth* hoping to relax during the five-day voyage. He had been working on a Twentieth Century Fox film and was in need of rest. On his left were two wealthy spinsters from Australia who were veteran travelers and had been everywhere. Their passage on Voyage 424 was one leg of a journey completely around the world.

The Captain of a great ocean liner is like a busy actor because he fills many roles. At one moment he may become

R.M.S. "Queen Elizabeth"

Juices: Pineapple - Apple - Tomato - Grapefruit

HORS D'ŒUVRES
Chilled Honeydew Melon   Chilled Crab Flake Cocktail
                    Smoked Salmon with Capers
                    Délice de Foie Gras, Alsacienne
Spanish Anchovies in Oil   Bismarck Herrings   Salade á la Russe
    Sardines in Oil   Œufs Tartare   Green Pepper Salad
            Olives: Queen - Spanish - Californian
            Crisp Hearts of Californian Celery

SOUP
Croûte-au-Pot   Crème Marie Stuart
                COLD: Crème Germiny

FISH
                Suprême de Fletan, Waleska
                Fillets of Boston Sole, Caprice
                Danish Brook Trout, Bretonne
            Escargots en Godette á la Bourguignonne

ENTREES
                Boned Sirloin of Beef, London House
                Braised Smoked Ox Tongue, Florentine

SPECIALITY
            Escalope de Veau, Parmigiana
Seasoned Escalope of Veal dipped in Whipped Eggs and Bread Crumbs
lightly cooked in Butter covered with sliced Mozzarelia and grated
Parmesan Cheese moistened with Tomato Sauce and sprinkled with
Paprika, baked in hot oven to complete cooking.

JOINT
    Roast Leg and Shoulder of Lamb, Mint Sauce, Red Currant Jelly

GRILL (to order)
Sirloin Steak, Hôtelier   Spring Chicken, Americain

RELEVE
            Roast Aylesbury Duckling, Apple Sauce
                    (Orange Salad)

D

SUGG

Melon

Crèm

Filet

Gigot d'Agne
Petits Pois

Souffl

Dessert

Your individual selectio
    our com

Passengers on specia
make known their re

Speciality Foods for

*This typical dinner menu was printed for Voyage 424 and used i
the Elizabeth's First Class Restaurant the day before the ship's a
rival in Europe.*

R

ENU

-appé

art

ice

e Menthe
mmes Persillées

ncy

Café

be purchased from
List

cially invited to
he Head Waiter

lable on request

FC

VEGETABLES
Garden Peas   French Beans
Fresh Leaf Spinach Romaine   Fried Egg Plant

Macaroni al Sugo

POTATOES
Persillées   au Gratin   Rissolées   French Fried

COLD BUFFET
Roast Ribs and Sirloin of Beef, Horseradish
Oxford Brawn   Galantine of Turkey   Roast Lamb, Mint Sauce
Rolled Ox Tongue   Baked York Ham   London Pressed Beef
Roast Chicken

SALADS
Hearts of Lettuce   Endive   Francaise
Pears and Cottage Cheese   Fresh Fruit   Escarole

DRESSINGS
Cream   Roquefort   Lemon   French

SWEETS
Soufflé Montmorency   Savarin aux Fruits, Chantilly
Pears Hélène
Compote of Apricots, Peaches and Pineapple—Whipped Cream
Petits Fours

ICE CREAM
Vanilla   Praline   Peach   Burnt Almond
(Hot Butterscotch Sauce)

SHERBET
Curacao

SAVOURIES
Welsh Rarebit   Croûte Windsor

FRESH FRUIT
Apples   Oranges   Pears   Bananas
Tangerines   Grapes   Pineapple   Plums

Dates   Almonds   Raisins   Crystallised Ginger   Figs

Assorted Cheeses

Tea (Hot or Iced)   Coffee (Hot or Iced)

involved with a leaky pipe that is upsetting some well-paying passenger. Or in his quarters he stoically accepts obsequious praise from someone who simply wants to meet the master of a great ship. Or the Captain may find himself escorting Her Majesty Queen Elizabeth, the Queen Mother, to the liner's cinema—as Commodore Marr did once. But through it all, he forever conducts the Captain's table where the master navigator often faces the storms and reefs of human personalities. Navigating the ship and the table requires vastly different skills, both important to mastering an ocean liner.

Commodore Marr chooses most often to play this role as a storyteller—with tales ranging from well-worn jokes to stories about his life at sea. He is best at the latter. That first evening of Voyage 424, the Commodore at one point explained he had once been Captain of the *Caronia,* a ship that he obviously remembers with fondness, for he took her on cruises for two years. "Whenever I leave a port, as we did today," said Commodore Marr, "I always remember a Miss Hobson who sailed with me on a round-the-world cruise of the *Caronia.* She was eighty-two years old and had recently inherited some money that obviously led her to take the cruise.

"We picked her up in England to make the world cruise, as I remember. When we stopped at Acapulco, Miss Hobson became the most famous passenger of the cruise. When she went ashore with the other passengers, she met a young Mexican who sold her a tour of the harbor in his small sailboat. The two of them set forth, but then the sailboat was becalmed.

"As it came time for us to leave, Miss Hobson's bedroom steward—the stewards are responsible for making sure that all passengers are on board at sailing time—reported the little old lady present, though she wasn't. Someone had told the steward that Miss Hobson was in the dining room, and he didn't check. Miss Hobson, to the contrary, was still in that Mexican's sailboat.

"As she saw the *Caronia* departing, she of course became thoroughly disturbed. Her Mexican sailor by this time was making way, for the wind had returned; so he set out after the *Caronia*. There we were, leaving Acapulco chased by a sailboat with a little old lady waving frantically at us. The passengers saw her, but didn't recognize the distant figure as Miss Hobson. They simply thought it was a tourist having a good time waving good-bye to the departing ship. The harder she waved, the harder they waved back.

"Miss Hobson was returned to the port where she cabled her travel agent. He contacted Cunard and we soon heard about our missing passenger. The company of course saw to it that Miss Hobson got to the next port before we did, and as the *Caronia* landed, there she was waiting for us."

As the Commodore told this story, his guests were waited upon in whispers by Rowland Hill, the Commodore's personal steward, several waiters, and a wine steward. The R.M.S. *Queen Elizabeth*'s first-class menu offered a wide selection of delectable food. It was possible to start the meal with any of a large choice of hors d'oeuvres, from honeydew melon to bluepoint oysters on the half shell, to smoked Irish salmon with capers, caviar, Bordeaux sardines, Bismarck herring, and Italian antipasto. Next came a selection of three fine soups: consommé Renaissance (chicken with a vegetable), Potage Busega (minestrone with slices of tripe), and cold cream of asparagus. Next was the fish course: broiled fillets of red snapper, Key West; poached fresh codling, Duglere; and cold split Maine lobster. But for the hearty eater the fish course was only the beginning. It was followed by an egg or meat course offering many choices. The specialty was Wiener Rostbraten (thin sirloin steak sautéed, and garnished with sautéed onions, German fried potatoes, grated horseradish, and watercress). Or one could order barbecued ham, a loin lamb chop, roast roulade of veal, calves' liver, chicken—or practically anything else that came to mind, whether it was on the menu or not.

"Cunard food has for many years been one of the most serious problems I have to face at sea," said Commodore Marr, as he made his selection that evening. "It's simply that everything is so good, and if I don't take care, my waistline will just grow and grow.

"My family at home worries about my eating habits more than anything else. You would think a sea captain's family might have other worries when he leaves for a voyage, but it's my waistline that seems to cause the most concern.

"I always remember what happened as I was departing for the long, round-the-world cruise on the *Caronia*. Just before leaving that particular morning I saw my daughter off to school. As I left her at the gate I said good-bye, to which she replied, 'Have a nice time, Daddy, but don't get too fat!' "

When the sumptuous meal had ended with fancy desserts for everyone, the Commodore and his guests took an elevator to the promenade deck where they had coffee and brandy in the *Queen Elizabeth*'s main lounge. Cabaret entertainment was about to start but the Commodore bid his friends good night and went directly up to the bridge.

Entering the wheelhouse, he walked with care until his eyes adjusted to the darkness. The *Elizabeth* was encountering heavy rain showers with gusting wind that made the ever-present howl rise and fall. The *Elizabeth*'s enormous hull was still pitching in the rough sea.

Commodore Marr conferred briefly with the officer of the watch, Junior First Finlay, who said that a few minutes before they had caught a brief glimpse of the Nantucket Shoals Lightship through the rain showers. The sighting was entered into the ship's log at 2139 (9:39 p.m. Eastern Standard Time). At that point, said Finlay, he had altered course as prescribed earlier by the Commodore. The liner had been turned just a few degrees to the north from a course almost due east. The new compass heading was 083 degrees.

The ship's Master went back to the radar enclosure where a seaman continued to watch the screen. Besides the mottled patterns of ocean waves a bright spot of light appeared in the top right quarter of the screen representing another vessel some 18 miles off the liner's starboard bow. The seaman and officers had been watching the spot for several minutes while employing an ingenious technique to learn where and how fast this other ship was going.

A couple of inches above the radar screen a convex glass cover is set so that the viewer must look through it to see the screen. When some special lights under the edge of the cover are snapped on, the screen is flooded with a dull illumination that creates a most useful optical illusion. Touching the cover gives the impression that you are touching the screen. The outer glass can be marked up with a grease pencil, and you appear to be drawing right on the screen. When the nearby ship's image was first seen, the seaman marked the spot with a dot. As the vessel steamed over the ocean, the spot of light moved slowly away from the dot. The seaman, with one eye on a clock in the radar enclosure, waited a couple of minutes and then placed a second dot over the light's new position. Thus he continued marking the slowly moving blob of light at equal time intervals until he had several dots which he connected with a line. The timed spacing of the dots and the connecting line told the men on the *Elizabeth*'s bridge two important facts about the distant ship. The line immediately revealed her course in relation to the *Elizabeth*. Then, with a measurement device included with the radar set, the seaman found the represented distance in miles between equally spaced dots. This figure provided all that was necessary to calculate the speed of the nearby ship.

She was not moving toward the *Queen Elizabeth* but on a

course taking her southeast of the liner. Had the dotted line pointed toward the *Elizabeth* or her course, the other vessel's speed would have then been important in determining whether or not the two ships were on collision courses.

From the radar enclosure, Commodore Marr moved to the lighted chart table where the latest weather map had been delivered for his surveillance. The storm stirring up the surrounding ocean remained ahead and was still moving slowly northeast. The *Elizabeth*'s Master believed he could still take the liner around the storm's bottom side to ride with the easterly winds.

Satisfied that all was well, Commodore Marr went down to his quarters close to 11 o'clock. It was a long day since arising early that morning in Greenwich, Connecticut, and commuting to his job at New York's Pier 92. In a half hour, he was in bed listening to the storm outside, and ready for sleep.

When passengers know the Commodore is absent from the bridge, especially in bad weather, an allegorical question often arises: "Who is minding the store?"

"I have an answer," says the Commodore, "that explains why the ship is in good hands when I am in the dining room, or in the lounge enjoying myself, or asleep in bed. I answer: 'There are nine other officers on this ship, all with master's certificates, all fully qualified to take command, and they're all waiting for me to retire from the job, or drop dead. Under the circumstances, they are bound to be doing their very best in behalf of the ship and the passengers' safety and comfort.' "

Chapter I X

Morning in the
Dining Room

A few minutes before 8 o'clock on the morning of April 14, Reginald H. Philp, the *Elizabeth*'s restaurant manager, stood in the grand foyer to the first-class dining room talking with the first customer of the day, a businessman from Wisconsin. The stately entryway paneled in English olive wood with ash burr has a large coat of arms of Her Majesty Queen Elizabeth carved in lime-tree wood. It is held by sculptured Elizabethan heralds over the tall doors leading to the dining room. Philp would open the doors promptly at 8 o'clock, though few passengers would enter. Most were still asleep, for it was not quite 7 a.m., New York time. The ship's clocks, however, had been advanced an hour at midnight, as they would be each twenty-four hours on the eastward voyage.

The sea had become very rough during the night, and the liner was pitching quite hard. Her rising and falling was very noticeable to the Wisconsin passenger who was on his first ocean voyage. But the motion didn't bother him as much as the creaking of the ship. It was especially evident here in the large empty foyer. With each rise and fall of the *Elizabeth* her interior woodwork sounded as though it were being twisted apart. It went *creeeeeeeak, creeeeeeeak, creeeeeeeak* with each pitch of the liner.

"The ship is making a lot of noise this morning," he said to Philp.

"I don't notice it," said Philp. "It's all part of a ship, and we grow used to the sound. In fact if she didn't creak I think I would refuse to sail on her. When you hear that sound, you know the ship is giving with the ocean. It means she's flexible. If she didn't creak she would strike me as a most brittle ship, and I wouldn't care to be with her."

Philp might have explained further that the *Queen Elizabeth*'s designers even planned for the liner to bend slightly in the middle in rough seas. The ship has four vertical expansion joints that extend from one side to the other and from the top deck down to the main deck. They are evenly spaced fore and aft so that above the main deck the liner is separated into five independent parts (except where they join at the bottom along the main deck). Below the joints the ship is completely connected from stem to stern. The joints make the long vessel more flexible and allow her to hog and sag without breaking as she rides up and down over the waves. (She bends up in the middle as she "hogs" and down as she "sags.")

The *Queen Elizabeth*'s flexibility is also increased by her being a riveted ship, whereas new ships are welded. Welding, claim some of the old hands on the *Elizabeth,* makes for a comparatively brittle ship whereas rivets make for overall flexibility because of the slight movements allowed at the hundreds of joints where steel plates come together in the hull. The riveted joints, say the old-timers, permit the ship to "mold to the ocean," and it thereby takes less of a beating from the powerful forces of the sea.

Such a ship, of course, creaks—but far less than would have been true had the *Elizabeth*'s interior woodwork not been specially joined with strips of felt between panels to prevent edges from rubbing directly against one another. But a man like Philp would never want the creaks stopped completely. The noise to him is a very secure sound, and without it he can't sleep well.

Like most of the *Queen* Ships' top staff the *Elizabeth*'s restaurant manager has spent his adult life on liners. "I have been at sea ever since May 20, 1922," says Philp, "when I went to work on the *Berengaria* as a messenger boy sailing between England and New York. Since then I have been on many ships. The *Aquitania, Sylvania, Britannic, Mauretania.* And of course I have sailed many times on the *Mary.* All of us have a place in our hearts for the *Mary.* A beautiful, beautiful ship."

In his career Philp worked up through the steward's ranks to become a headwaiter and then to being one of the Cunard Line's top restaurant managers. The line's larger ships have restaurant managers over the headwaiters. Smaller liners have only headwaiters. On the *Elizabeth* Philp is in charge of all dining-room stewards in all classes, and during mealtimes he directs the service of the first-class dining room, which is the largest afloat. The big room, which has seated 865 people at once and provided them with the most luxurious kind of dinner service, had three headwaiters with about ninety stewards on Voyage 424.

"We try to have one waiter to every six first-class passengers," explained Philp. "There are two other large dining rooms in cabin and tourist classes, each with a large number of waiters, but fewer per passenger. And then up in the stern of the ship we have the Verandah Grill, an exclusive restaurant for first-class passengers. In first class, of course, your meals go with the cost of your passage, but in the Verandah Grill they cost an extra pound for lunch or dinner. Celebrities who wish to avoid the crowds of the main dining room are likely to go to the Grill for their meals."

Besides directing the *Elizabeth*'s large, luxurious dining room for three daily meals, the restaurant manager conducts a training program. He spends a lot of time on the liner with young boys who are learning to be dining-room stewards. Philp even gives them lecture classes between meals on all that is necessary to offer the *Elizabeth*'s dining services.

"One of the main subjects I stress with my boys is hygiene," Philp explained. "This is a tight community that we live and work in. They learn that, above all, there is to be a minimum of handling chinaware, silverware, and glasses. They learn how to fold napkins so as to handle them very little. I then give the new boys a complete course on the meals from beginning to end. What to serve first, what comes next, and so on. How to handle every item of food with a spoon or fork.

"After the lectures, the boys are started out serving water and rolls, and then clearing the tables. The first individual act of a boy is carving smoked salmon. I give lessons on carving all kinds of meat and fish, but I start them on the salmon. I can watch a boy with salmon and tell you a lot about his future. How he goes about carving salmon—it's difficult to cut well, thin and even—it tells me a great deal about what he can do.

"A good boy can become a full-fledged waiter in a year.

He starts in tourist class and works up to first class. Then, when he is good enough to take a job as head of staff, he goes back to tourist in charge of waiters. Once more he works his way up to first class in charge of waiters. All the boys keep going through the same upward steps—tourist to first class—until they may even become headwaiters under me in the first-class dining room."

The man who aspires to be a top waiter on a liner like the *Elizabeth* must be able to discuss a wide variety of special foods, as well as to serve them. Even the breakfast menu is one seldom equaled anywhere. For the first breakfast of Voyage 424 the menu was long and detailed as usual. The listings began with eighteen selections of juices or fruit and eleven kinds of cereal, followed by a specialty—"onion soup, gratinée." Next were two kinds of fish: fried fillet of plaice, or salt ling fish with cream. Eggs and omelettes were listed in fifteen different styles. Of course, there were bacon, ham, and sausage—but one could also order tripe, roast sirloin of beef with horseradish, rolled ox tongue, or fresh brawn.

The passenger ambitious enough to rise for breakfast could also enjoy a salad with hearts of lettuce, radishes, sliced tomatoes, and spring onions. Then an American passenger might even be surprised to find an item in the menu's middle always on breakfast menus back home: griddle cakes, buckwheat cakes, or waffles with Vermont maple syrup. Last of all, the *Elizabeth*'s menu listed a dozen different breads and rolls, with a choice of preserves, and sixteen different kinds of beverages from various teas and coffees to yoghurt.

The dining room was open that morning, but no more than two dozen passengers appeared for breakfast, although the main kitchen was busy sending meals to the cabins. Most of the time Philp simply waited by the main doors to seat the few people who came into the room. Sometimes he stood for a few minutes by a table talking with a passenger as the person ordered and ate a leisurely meal. One man knew Philp very well, for the passenger had been traveling on Atlantic liners three decades. "Over the years, Reginald," the man said, "you must have waited on a lot of famous people in these dining rooms."

"Oh, yes, I can remember serving a great many of the famous," said Philp. "I even recall seeing the Prince of Wales on his first trip to America on the *Berengaria*. I served Jack Dempsey when he went abroad on his wedding trip with Estelle Taylor. And Gertrude Ederle as she was going to America after her famous swim of the English Channel.

"And there have been many movie stars. Charlie Chaplin and Paulette Goddard traveled with me. Oh, I could go on and on with such names of the famous. Henry Ford, I served. And I helped with parties given by Elsa Maxwell as she traveled to and from Europe."

After breakfast Philp remained in the dining room inspecting the tables which had been set for lunch. Each one had thirteen pieces of silverware to a setting. The restaurant manager made sure each piece was precisely in place. He looked very carefully to see that none of the silver or glassware showed any sign of contact with a waiter's hand. It is supposed to be handled only with a cloth or napkin. He also noted how the passengers' napkins had been folded and placed on the tables. Philp asks that they be prepared with a simple straight fold, rather than making them stand as a cone.

Satisfied that his tables were ready for lunch, the restaurant manager walked through the main kitchen, down to the working alleyway, and back to his quarters. There he reread some mail from his family. Philp and his wife keep a home in a village near Southampton. They have raised three children and now have six grandchildren whom the restaurant manager seldom sees.

Chapter X

Navigating the Storm

That morning Commodore Marr arose long before breakfast.
At 1:30 a.m. his concern for the weather caused him to get up,
put on a robe and slippers, and visit the bridge. With Senior
First Officer Munro, on the 12-to-4 watch, he studied the charts
and the latest radio weather reports, all of which still supported his opinion that it would be best to skirt the southern
side of the Nantucket storm.

The Commodore returned to bed and slept until nearly 7
a.m. when he was awakened by the wind, which had increased

in intensity. Without lifting his head from the pillow, he
could tell by the sound and feel of his great ship that the wind
had shifted and was now driving the sea almost straight at the
liner. She was being battered badly by wind and spray, vibrat-
ing as she took one big wave after another, and pitching much
more than before. He unhappily suspected that the low-pressure system had not moved northeast on the Atlantic as he had
anticipated. Had it done so, the wind would be shifting to the
port quarter and eventually to the stern. If the low had not
moved as expected, the *Queen Elizabeth* could very well be
moving into the northwestern side of the system where she
would encounter headwinds from the north-northeast.

Commodore Marr got out of bed and hurried up to the
bridge in his robe and slippers. The ship, he found, was plowing into a heavy sea whose large waves were marching one at a
time almost directly at the liner's prow. The Commodore then
found that the usually up-to-the-minute weather data were in-
complete, for heavy radio static was preventing the reception
of late meteorological information. But the wind direction, the
look of the sea, and the nature of the clouds told the Commodore all he needed to know about the forces of nature in
this rough vicinity. His assumptions, made while still in bed,
were supported by what he saw through the rain-covered
wheelhouse windows. Outside, everything was drenched by
gray rain and salt-water spray driven by the wind. The impos-
ing bow of the *Elizabeth,* her open main deck swept with rushing floods of sea water, was slowly rising and falling as she
cut through the heavy seas. Once in a while, as the liner
dropped over the crest of an exceptionally large wave, tons of
spray were thrown high into the air.

The quartermaster at the helm held the ship straight on
the designated course of 083 degrees. But the waves ahead
shoved the 83,000-ton liner to and fro and continually made
him counter the forces by skillful handling of the wheel. It

required a concentration so taxing that he was much relieved every half hour to turn the job over to the second quartermaster.

These were moments to think well of the *Queen* Ships' designers and builders who, far back in the twenties and thirties, made these great machines of the North Atlantic for the worst that any ocean could offer. Here in the 1960's the magnificent *Elizabeth* was performing in full with all of her plates, planks, beams, and rivets. With each swell her beautifully raked prow rose majestically; then she settled, again, slowly, beautifully down into the sea, through the trough to meet the next swell. As she descended, the enormous force of the ocean was absorbed along the plates all down her hull, a fifth of a mile to her stern. In these seconds the sound and feel of the sea were relayed to all her decks and departments. Furniture shuddered and the wood paneling drawn from all over the earth groaned as the *Elizabeth* "molded to the ocean." In this sea, long passageways paralleling the hull were uphill then downhill walks, and one had the feeling that the tubelike hallways gave a twist as the liner drove against the sea. Meanwhile, thirty-seven large public rooms rose, fell, and shook with the ocean as the largest liner on earth pressed forward. In seas like this, one quickly recognizes that the soul of these tons and tons of iron and wood is something left there by the workmen who faired this ship during her construction on the Clyde in the 1930's.

From what the Commodore could see he seriously questioned the course on which the liner stood. He spent the better part of the next half hour reviewing his navigational plans. He and Chief Officer Arbuckle studied the charts and discussed the problem at length, though anyone listening in could tell the responsibility was on the man in the lounging robe and slippers.

The Commodore, as we learned earlier, had intended to

follow the North Atlantic Lane Route, Track B, recom-
mended for that time of year. This meant continuing east-
northeast until crossing the meridian of 47 degrees west at 40
degrees and 30 minutes of north latitude. Following Track B
the *Elizabeth* would then stay just south of a great circle to the
southwestern tip of the British Isles. The Lane Routes (which
include tracks A, B, C, D, E, F, and G, from south to north)
are popularly known as highways of the sea. They were agreed
upon long ago by many of the large steamship companies, including Cunard, in the North Atlantic Track Agreement.
The tracks supposedly keep ships from colliding as they proceed in opposing directions. Some lanes are only for eastbound ships; others are restricted to westbound vessels, and a
third group are used for both directions, except that eastbound ships stay a few miles south of the track line while
westbound stay north. Track B is this last type.

Although the lane system was designed for a good purpose, it is not as effective as it could be, mainly because all
vessels do not follow them. While one steamship follows a lane
route because her company is party to the agreement, a big
tanker may ignore the tracks because her company is not.
Therefore no ship's master dare proceed along a track as
though all were clear ahead. To be safe he must assume the
lanes are nonexistent and rely upon his radar, his eyes, ears,
and every other safeguard to avoid collision. But this is by no
means difficult with modern navigational aids, especially with
the kind of radar on the *Elizabeth*. Another problem is that
storms certainly do not respect the North Atlantic Lane
Routes. The greatest storm of the century could settle directly
over a leading lane, and the master who then stuck to the
course would certainly be guilty of using bad judgment.

And that's somewhat the spot in which Commodore Marr
now found himself. The Track B course might take his ship
and passengers right into the center of the storm. But before

concluding that this was definitely so, the Commodore decided to wait for a short while in hopes that the ship's radio
room would receive some clarifying weather data. He went to
his quarters where he dressed and ate a light breakfast before
returning to the bridge about 8:15. The radio room was still
having no success, and there had been no visible change in the
wind and weather. The Commodore was now certain that the
low-pressure system was sitting still in the Atlantic almost directly ahead. The present course might very well take the
Elizabeth into the center of the storm, so he decided to change
his overall plan for crossing the Atlantic, and began working
out a new route.

A review of the latest available weather charts, showing
the storm the night before, indicated that the way to avoid the
low-pressure system was to go up and around it by following
the Canadian Lane Route, Track F. Mid-April would be considered early for the use of Track F, but this year's ice reports
revealed that F was clear. Therefore, in view of the immediate
Atlantic weather patterns, the Canadian track was undoubtedly the safest possible course for the Elizabeth's Voyage
424.

After some time looking over the chart and discussing it
with his officers, the Commodore gave an order for a change in
course to a northeast heading that would take the ship toward
Cape Race on Newfoundland's Avalon Peninsula. Track F
begins near Cape Race. Just before changing course, the Elizabeth was about 400 miles east of New York.

"Ask them to put out the fins," said the Commodore to
Junior First Officer Finlay, who telephoned the order to the
engineering department.

Beneath her water line, the Queen Elizabeth has four
gyroscopically controlled stabilizer fins, two on each side of
the ship spaced a couple hundred feet apart. When not in use,
they are withdrawn from the sea to four watertight housings

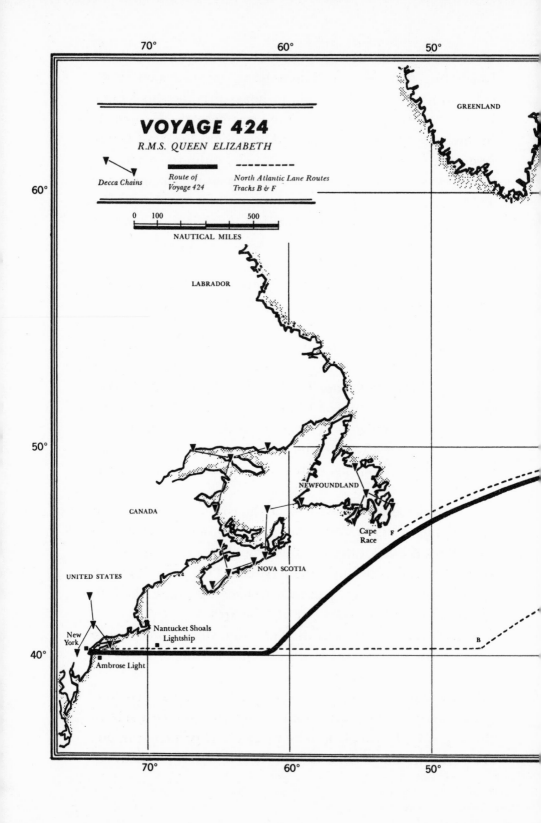

VOYAGE 424

R.M.S. QUEEN ELIZABETH

Decca Chains

Route of
Voyage 424

North Atlantic Lane Routes
Tracks B & F

0   100   500

NAUTICAL MILES

GREENLAND

LABRADOR

NEWFOUNDLAND

CANADA

Cape
Race

F

NOVA SCOTIA

UNITED STATES

New
York

Nantucket Shoals
Lightship

B

Ambrose Light

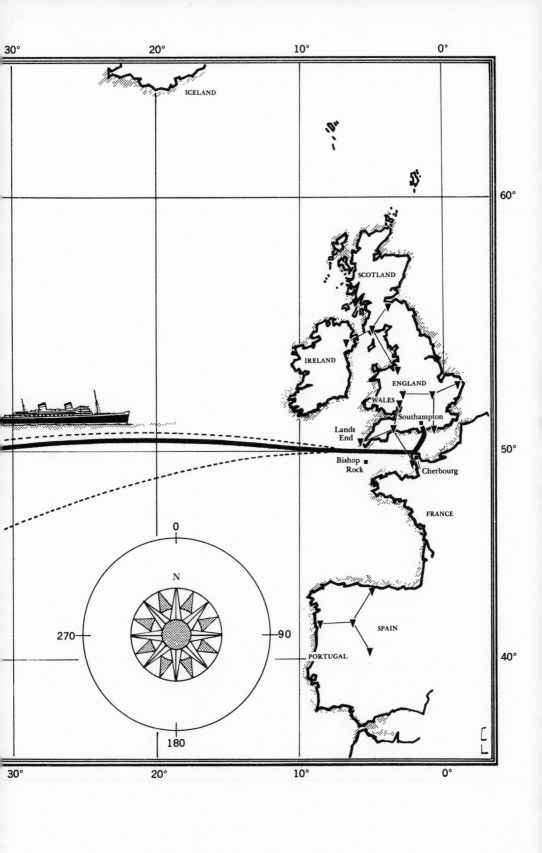

just inside the hull, and when needed, they are projected by powerful hydraulic rams. With her fins out, the liner, in a sense, has little wings that work on the principle of ailerons to reduce her rolling in a rough sea (though they don't reduce pitching). When the ocean is such that it would roll the liner 20 degrees from her upright position, the fins can reduce it to about five degrees. Of course, they are limited in their power to stop the *Queen Elizabeth* from rolling in an extremely heavy sea, though they help even in the worst of conditions.

When the first *Queen* Ship, the *Mary,* set out on her maiden voyage, May 27, 1936, it was assumed that here was a vessel so heavy that roll would never be a problem. She had no handrails in the corridors, nor was her furniture fastened down. That summer the assumption seemed to prove true, but on an October crossing of the Atlantic, the notion was suddenly shattered. The new *Queen* ran into a storm with 55-mile-an-hour gales, and at one point she suddenly dipped to one side. Some of the crew felt her going "slowly, down and down and down," and they thought she was never coming back. People were even thrown out of bed by the roll. She did come back, of course, but her heavy hull, once set into motion, kept her rocking, back and forth. Passengers became hysterical, and many were injured. Her master, to settle her down, had to reduce her speed by roughly half. He, his crew, and passengers learned in a hurry that the designers had been wrong in thinking that weight could prevent roll. In Southampton the liner picked up joiners and carpenters who spent the next voyage fastening down furniture and installing handrails for passengers to grab should they fall. For years thereafter the *Mary* was known as a "roller" until she, along with her sister ship, acquired a set of fins.

Pitch and roll are old and natural enemies to Commodore Marr, and he has often been forced to take both at once. However, if he has a choice, years of experience with passenger liners have taught him to prefer roll. Pitch, rather than roll, he blames as the primary cause of seasickness. The rising and falling of the vessel in line with her direction of movement seems to disorient people as they walk in the passageways, most of which run fore and aft. The person without sea legs who takes a forward step and fails to find the deck where he expects it to be is often left with a queasy feeling. Too much of this and the Commodore's social problems increase with a liner full of sick, unhappy passengers.

Roll has its hazards, as well. The trouble arises as a passenger walks parallel to the ship's course, and a roll suddenly forces the person in an opposing direction. Then the traveler unaccustomed to the ways of the sea may find himself sprawling on the deck or bouncing his head off a bulkhead. To help people counter such falls, the *Elizabeth*'s passageways are lined with grab rails. In heavy seas, special "rolling ropes" are stretched across open public rooms and foyers so that a person thrown off balance has something to catch and prevent a tumble. When the ropes are up, passengers have the benefit of extra exercise, for the waist-high lines often have to be ducked under or walked around.

With his fins out and his course changed, Commodore Marr felt he had gained at least one advantage for his passengers' comfort. On the previous heading, with the sea coming directly at the prow, they were afflicted by the ship's pitching, for which he had no remedy. On the new heading, the sea was coming from off the starboard bow, producing a roll which the fins could remedy. But when all this was done, the great liner was still not riding well. There was some pitch, and the fins were unable to stop the roll completely. But it wasn't too bad, and even a landlubber most susceptible to mal de mer could pretty much forget he was riding across the world's roughest ocean during a bad storm. At any rate, most such passengers had already prepared for a rough ride by visiting the ship's doctors for motion-sickness drugs. These were offered in the form of pills or a more lasting application, by injection. In either case the drugs work on the brain's vomiting center to prevent the dreadful symptoms that have spoiled trips at sea for ages and ages past.

All morning hundreds of passengers walked along the enclosed promenade decks and looked through the long rows of windows, fascinated by the rough sea through which the liner was plowing. Many of them, with their legs and laps wrapped in blankets, sat in traditional fashion in deck chairs where they read books or chatted with one another. Late in the morning, deck attendants offered beef tea and crackers, also traditional on a British liner.

The people who operate ships like the *Queen Elizabeth* naturally never use expensive advertising space to illustrate their liners sailing through rough weather. The advertisements feature open-deck scenes with people relaxing, playing games, or swimming in a sunlit swimming pool against a brilliant blue sea in the background. These scenes are a part of many ocean voyages, but seldom on a North Atlantic crossing in April, when the weather alternates between winter and summer. Then the passengers are often limited to the enclosed parts of the ship—which of course have swimming pools, games of all kinds, and a wide variety of entertainment such as concerts, motion pictures, singers, and dancers. But stormy voyages have a special interest. Riding a great ship through a rough sea is a real adventure, even if experienced in a luxury liner's plush surroundings. All of us it seems have something of the mariner in our blood. On Voyage 424, the passengers were certainly involved with the navigational problems. Bedroom stewards, waiters, elevator operators, and deck attendants were constantly asked for information about the ship and her course. Where are we now? How long will this

storm last? Is this the storm that damaged the *Michelangelo?*
Do you call this a rough sea?

The crew offered many answers, some with great detail
and with a manner of expertise, while others were perfunc-
tory. Of course, the real story was found only on the navigation bridge where the officers and their quartermasters fought
with the ocean and the winds moment by moment. Their aim
was to run the massive liner through the storm in such a way
as to draw the least attention to the weather. For decades those
who have owned and operated ocean liners have felt they
should avoid making their voyages hair-raising adventures,
and instead try to approximate life ashore. This was reflected
in an early description of the *Queen Mary* published by a
trade magazine, *Architect and Building News.*

"For the public there is only one imaginative criterion by
which the quality of a great liner is assured and that is the
degree to which land conditions are reproduced afloat.

"The entire romance of a ship design resides in the sensa-
tional contrast between the cold frightening inhumanity of
the steel hull cutting its way through the ocean and the cosy
intimate warmth of the interior in which all the minutes of
ordinary life are reproduced. . . ."

Chapter XI

Inspection

"Sometimes I compare my job as master of the *Queen Elizabeth* with that of running a factory," says Commodore Marr. "The ship is like a factory with over a thousand employees, who seldom go home. You must house, feed, and entertain them. You must provide them with the best of medical services. At the same time you may have twice that many people as passengers who are with you around the clock. They have to be housed, fed, and entertained, also. And of course the passengers present additional problems related to their comforts. As if that were not enough, you are meanwhile trying to sail the largest ship in the world across the roughest ocean on earth."

When the Commodore finished his navigational work on the bridge that morning, he hurried back to his quarters for the first full staff meeting of Voyage 424. Though the *Queen Elizabeth* had left her New York dock at noon the day before (April 13), this day (April 14) was considered the first at sea. In a few minutes, his top staff members arrived and were seated in the circle of comfortable chairs in the Commodore's quarters. The ship's Master pulled his desk chair into the circumference of the circle.

"Well, gentlemen," said Commodore Marr, "you will be happy to know that we got off to a very good start yesterday. We departed from New York [Ambrose] at two o'clock instead of two-thirty as estimated. We may need that half hour before we get through. Our required speed is an average 28.42 knots, but we'll be lucky if we can keep 27 today.

"As we were leaving yesterday, a storm was off Nantucket, and it looked as though we could go to the south of it, but the weather changed in the night. I was just on the bridge, and we decided to try our luck around to the north of the storm. We will have to keep our eyes on it and do the best we can.

"The fins are out, as you know, Mr. Philip [the Chief Engineer]. We'll take them in again as soon as possible.

"We have an ETA [Estimated Time of Arrival] Cherbourg at Monday noon, ship's time. We are due to leave there at four o'clock."

"Any shore leave for the crew?" asked Staff Captain Storey.

"I think we had better say no to that," replied the Commodore. "They've been wanting to buy perfume ashore—prices are particularly good right now, I guess—but it's such a short and busy stop that I think best we don't allow shore leave."

The meeting moved from subject to subject, some large and involved, others comparatively minor. The Commodore appeared equally interested in all the problems, whether they involved the ship's course or the comfort of a tourist-class passenger whose washbasin leaked.

"How are we doing with the tea bags?" said Commodore Marr to the *Elizabeth*'s Chief Steward, J. R. Smith, who is in charge of all catering services from the food departments to the care of the passengers' cabins.

"They are working out quite well, sir," said Smith. "They still plug up the drains but we can fish them out."

This was a problem that had long bothered the *Queen Elizabeth*'s engineers. Serving tea on a British liner is, of course, of major importance. Cunard, until recently, had purchased the best grades in bulk. But when the teapots were emptied, loose wet tea leaves often plugged up sink drains so badly that they had to be taken apart for cleaning. At long last, the solution turned out to be the packaging of the finest teas in teabags. Should they catch in sink drains they can be fished out without the services of an engineer.

The staff meeting concluded with a discussion of the Commodore's reception that evening. It was to be a pre-dinner party in one of the large public rooms where the Commodore would meet all first-class passengers who cared to come. During the discussion the Commodore held a passenger list on which the first-class travelers were divided up among the *Elizabeth*'s top officers to make sure that the passengers were well cared for at the party. Chief Engineer R. E. Philip was to be responsible for one group, and Purser Pritchard and his staff pursers, K. B. Allen and B. Jenkins, were responsible for another. Groups were assigned to the ship's Principal Medical Officer, Dr. F. W. A. Fosbery, and to Chief Steward

Smith. The officers already knew many of their assigned passengers from previous voyages.

"Captain Storey, you know Mr. and Mrs. So-and-so,"
Commodore Marr would say. "Can you see to them?"

"Oh, I met them years ago on the *Mary*," Captain Storey
would answer. "A lovely couple. He's a professor, I believe. I
look forward to seeing them again."

"I don't need to emphasize to you gentlemen," concluded
the Commodore, "that we're as much in the hotel business
these days as in the shipping business. Cunard wants us to
make each crossing more and more like a cruise. You know
our slogan, 'Getting there is half the fun.' There's a lot of
stress on this, so it is up to us to put it to work."

With no more business to conduct, the Commodore
abruptly ended the meeting at exactly 10:30 by whirling
his chair around to his desk and saying, "Thank you, gentlemen!"—at which signal everyone left.

In less than a half hour the same officers assembled on the
Queen Elizabeth's R Deck outside the first-class restaurant
where they waited to start the daily inspection of the ship. In a
few minutes Commodore Marr, wearing his white-topped officer's cap and brown leather gloves, stepped off a nearby elevator, cut through the group of officers, and headed for a door
behind them.

"I will take the after catering quarters this morning, gentlemen," he said as he passed through the group. He was
joined by Chief Master at Arms Harold Bretherton who was
in his dress uniform and armed with a large flashlight.

The Commodore's announcement was followed by a similar one from Staff Captain Storey, who said he would inspect
the *Elizabeth*'s first-class quarters. Each officer down the chain
of command picked one of the remaining sections of the ship
and departed to carry out an inspection. The liner was thus
divided up into six sections, each of which receives an inspec-

tion from some top officer every morning at sea. The sections include first-, cabin-, and tourist-class passenger accommodations, the catering accommodations, the seamen's quarters, and the ship's kitchens and storerooms. No officer can be certain about which of the six sections he will inspect, for the Commodore, who has first choice, never reveals his plans until he meets the officers and the inspection starts. The Staff Captain, who has second choice, doesn't reveal his plans—and so on down the chain of command. Thus none of the staff can be certain when his part of the ship will be inspected by the top officers.

From R Deck Commodore Marr went down some steps to the working alleyway where meat, vegetables, linen, and a thousand other supplies are continually on the move. He walked briskly back through the ship, passing storerooms, the bakery, kitchens, butcher shops, and the other busy areas which are home base for the liner's many services. As he walked with his long strides, he occasionally said hello to top staff people.

"I haven't seen the Jones boys," said the Commodore to the Chief Master at Arms. "Are they well and at work?"

"Fine as usual," answered Bretherton, who was short of breath trying to keep up with the liner's Master. The Jones boys, two men named Jones though not related, are the ship's butcher and baker.

The after catering accommodations, to which the Commodore was proceeding, are the quarters occupied by the liner's waiters, bedroom stewards, deck attendants, bartenders, and others who serve passengers. They are on three decks at the *Queen Elizabeth*'s stern with some of the cabins directly above the liner's rudder and propellers. En route Commodore Marr left the working alleyway and crossed the "pig 'n whistle deck," a comparatively open area with a number of tables and benches along its sides. Several men were seated around the tables drinking beer, bottled sodas, tea, or coffee. The pig 'n whistle deck is where crew members spend their leisure hours. To the Englishmen aboard a British liner this deck replaces their pubs ashore. In fact, many land-based pubs are called "pig 'n whistle," a name which comes from the old practice of instructing the boy sent to draw ale to whistle all the while the bung or peg was out of the barrel, so that he couldn't swallow any of the ale; in other words, to pull the peg and whistle.

Beyond this area, the Commodore came to the catering accommodations. He and Bretherton were joined by the "glory-hole steward," whose job it was to take care of his fellow stewards' quarters. In the nautical slang of the past this area was referred to as the "glory hole."

"How is the air-conditioning working?" asked the Commodore, as he and the steward began inspecting the cabins. The air-conditioning in this area of the ship had been installed just prior to the *Elizabeth*'s departure from England as part of an effort to improve crew quarters.

"I have had no complaints," said the steward. "A few men have tried to close off the outlets, but I asked them not to do it."

"They mustn't," said the Commodore. "The engineers tell me that if the system is to remain in balance and maintain the temperature at a nice comfortable sixty-eight or seventy degrees, all the outlets must be free to work. They spent a lot of time balancing up the system. We can't throw it off by shutting off ventilators."

Commodore Marr walked rapidly from cabin to cabin, inspecting them for cleanliness and for need of repairs. The passageways were lined with men who waited outside their quarters until the inspection was complete. Occasionally the Commodore would recognize an old hand among the crewmen, and he would linger for a word or two with the man.

In one cabin he found a steward in bed ill, so he stopped for a minute to talk.

The *Queen Elizabeth*'s caterers' accommodations were of great concern to the ship's Master. Their basic construction made it difficult, and in many cases impossible, to provide the privacy or even the square footage per man that the Commodore felt the crew members deserved.

"When the *Elizabeth* was built," he says, "working conditions were not considered as important as they are today. So the caterers' accommodations have cabins originally designed to accommodate as many as a dozen or more men. Today's stewards won't live under those conditions. You can't blame them. They want private or semiprivate quarters. They can get them on the new ships because the designers have had to account for changes in our outlook on working conditions. Meanwhile, we have to work with some pretty difficult situations in the *Elizabeth*. The crew quarters—some of them fitted right into the main structure of the ship—can't be renovated easily. You can't tear out partitions or even add new ones in many cases. One way to improve their lot would be to give the crew space taken from the passenger accommodations, but that would cut down on revenue and a ship like this couldn't afford the loss of income. Instead we've tried to distribute the men so that there are fewer per cabin. Modern equipment in the kitchens and elsewhere has allowed us to cut down on the number of employees so that we now have fewer to quarter, which is a help. Some of the big cabins that once held a dozen or so men now have only seven or eight.

"This is the kind of problem that truly ages a ship. She really ages socially and economically. It isn't that the hull or superstructure grows tired and weak. It's a matter of the ship not being able to compete economically with other ships and other means of transportation.

"Crew quarters are an integral part of this competition.

Either the men get what their fellow workers on other ships get or you're in trouble."

In one of the crew lavatories Commodore Marr stopped for a careful look around the washbowls where a leak had discolored and loosened up some new white paint. He discussed what might be done to fix the unattractive area, then ordered that it receive prompt attention.

Outside in a passageway the Commodore saw that the deck covering had worn through, and he asked that it be repaired. "The original covering they used on these decks was the best I ever saw," said the *Elizabeth*'s Master. "You can still find it in some places. It's the dark red material. This new stuff doesn't last nearly as long."

The inspection completed, the Commodore thanked the glory-hole steward, made his way back up to R Deck, and then walked forward through the liner to return to his quarters. As he walked across the pig 'n whistle deck his foot slipped on something that had been spilled on the deck. It caused him to lose his balance and fall so that he landed hard on his back and side. Men rushed from every direction to help him up, but before they reached him the Commodore was on his feet brushing off and straightening his blue uniform and hat. He said nothing, but simply mustered all of his dignity and walked off the pig 'n whistle deck. Behind him a group of stewards studied the deck and argued over who made the mess that caused the top man's tumble.

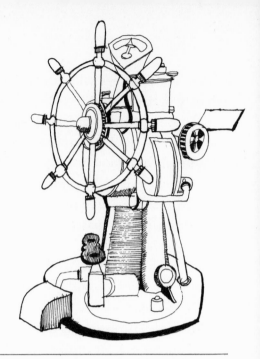

Chapter XII

A Long Day
for the
Commodore

Before noon the *Queen Elizabeth*'s radio room was able to receive a weather report from the United States, and an up-to-date weather map of the Atlantic was being prepared. Meanwhile the sea became progressively worse. Despite the ship's extended fins and her new course at an angle to the oncoming waves, the ocean was having its way with the liner more and more. The pitching was again increasing, and there was more roll than the fins could cope with successfully. In these midday hours of April 14 the *Elizabeth* encountered some of the largest waves of Voyage 424, often 20 feet or higher. At times the liner's sharply raked prow rose and fell as much as 60 to 75 feet as she pushed forward through the turbulent ocean.

It was astonishing how much sea water was thrown around by the world's largest liner forcing her way full steam through these seas. For a few moments she would generate comparatively little spray, but then her rising and falling prow would hit the right wave or combination of waves and send tons of spray flying in heavy, gray curtains toward the sky. The spray would rise a hundred feet above the ocean in front of the liner and appear to fly directly back at the wheelhouse, though it was really a case of the liner racing forward to meet the water. As this occurred, the bow seemed to dip under the ocean's surface.

The people most affected by the *Elizabeth*'s motion were the members of her crew whose accommodations were in the forecastle forward near the bow and right under the main deck, which was now shipping tons of water. In their cabins it was like riding an elevator that shuttled from top to bottom of a building, six or more stories. The descent often came with a crash as Niagaras of sea water struck the steel hull's riveted sides. But all the movement and noise was so familiar to most of the crewmen from hundreds of ocean voyages that it was now just routine. Many who were off duty slept peacefully, rising and falling in their bunks in cadence with the ocean waves. To these men, whose duties may rudely demand wakefulness at all hours of the night and day, the roughest sea only rocks their cradle to the lullaby of water clashing with steel.

Far above in the wheelhouse, Commodore Marr watched Senior Third Officer Dootson complete the weather chart from the radioed data. While the swirling isobars were drawn, the *Elizabeth*'s Master studied the evolving patterns which confirmed his earlier assumptions that the storm off Nantucket had definitely lost much of its headway toward the northeast. When the isobars were all completed, the navigational officer plotted a straight line for a few inches across part of the ocean to represent the *Elizabeth*'s present course. At a point along the line, he drew a small cross in a circle to indicate the liner's present position. Commodore Marr, rubbing his chin with his right hand, studied the new chart in consternation. The immediate storm had become a larger system than was indicated the night before. The *Elizabeth* was now about 300 miles west-northwest of the low-pressure center, but its effects were reaching the liner's position and considerably beyond, as clearly proven by the heavy seas she was encountering.

The Commodore realized now that his ship would suffer rough seas far into the night, and he should definitely remain close to the bridge. He immediately telephoned the ship's Purser, Fergus Pritchard, to cancel the Captain's reception planned that evening, and he sent a note to Restaurant Manager Philp, explaining that his guests should still be served a special dinner he had ordered, though he would be absent.

He returned to the weather chart and soon concluded it might be well to change the ship's course even a little more to the north from her current heading. The few degrees' change would add a few miles to the voyage, but it would swing the *Elizabeth* out toward the fringes of the bad-weather system where the wind and sea would likely be less violent. What he lost in miles, figured the Commodore, he might gain in smoother, steadier sailing. Also, the fuel consumed could be less than if he held to the shorter course, but plowed through rougher seas.

"Bring her around to zero-four-zero," said the Commodore to Chief Officer Arbuckle, now on watch.

"Zero-four-zero!" called out Arbuckle to the helmsman who slowly brought the *Elizabeth* around to port. Meanwhile Arbuckle erased "050" and wrote "040" on a small chalk board hung on the wall at the front of the wheelhouse directly in view of the quartermaster at the helm. The liner had been steaming on a 50-degree heading since the Commodore had made up his mind to pass the storm to the north rather than to the south. He planned to hold the new course for several hours, then slowly bring her back to the east again.

At this time, some twenty-seven hours after dropping the Sandy Hook pilot, the *Queen Elizabeth* had sailed about 600 miles. She was almost due east of Yarmouth, Nova Scotia, and was pointed directly at the easternmost tip of Newfoundland. The 10-degree change in course brought the oncoming waves around even more to the starboard, and, as the Commodore had anticipated, they increased the *Elizabeth*'s rolling to the point where her fins seemed quite ineffective.

"I think we had better put up the rolling lines," said the Commodore. "I am not sure they really need be up, but let's be on the safe side."

Arbuckle telephoned the order to the deck department, and in a few minutes, seamen were stringing the lines from point to point in all the public rooms.

"A fine end to my reception," said the Commodore. "When the rolling lines go up it dampens spirits in general. It's a sign for most all the elderly ladies to go to bed."

Arbuckle laughed as he answered, "Yes, sir!"

"I always enjoy the reception," said the Commodore. "It gives me a chance to meet everyone and try getting the passengers together so they will enjoy the trip more."

The sea remained rough late into the night. At one point, the *Elizabeth* cut through a snowstorm that temporarily bleached her dark decks with a coat of melting snow. Around midnight, however, it became evident to the Commodore that he was outdistancing the worst of the storm. The wind and sea, though rough indeed, were not nearly as violent as in the late afternoon and early evening. The wind direction in relation to the liner also indicated that the *Elizabeth* was gaining in her attempt to detour around the worst of the storm.

All that evening the Commodore remained either on the navigation bridge or in his nearby quarters where he was served an early dinner by his valet, Rowland Hill. He ate alone, an hour or so before his guests in the dining room enjoyed the special meal that he had ordered for the Captain's table, where the head seat remained empty. Indeed, an unwritten law of the sea imposes a penalty on anyone other than the ship's Master taking the chair. It says that the offender has to buy drinks for all the dining-room stewards. The Commodore's absence was no surprise, for the guests suspected the weather would keep their host on the bridge. The fact was confirmed by the Commodore's valet. "The Commodore," said Hill, "begs to be forgiven, but he will not be able to join you this evening. The weather is nasty and he is staying on the bridge.

"As I think he told you, the Commodore arranged a special dinner which was to follow his reception. He sent word down to the chef that the dinner was to be presented as planned, though he would have to be absent. He asked me to supervise the service of the dinner and make sure that everyone is well pleased."

Throughout the meal the Commodore's steward directed the waiters, busboys, and wine steward with meticulous attention to detail. The meal began with Russian caviar rolled in thin strips of Nova Scotia salmon. A young man sliced the pink fish on a portable table as Hill critically observed the performance. With his arms folded over his chest, his head held high, and his eyes cast down toward the carving knife, Hill stood stiffly at attention a foot from the table until the salmon was ready to serve.

Rowland Hill is part of the Cunard Line's concern with preserving the life and times of what Americans often feel right or wrong is the English way of life. Hill is a professional butler who makes a career of serving British royalty or highly placed persons such as Commodore Marr. Before joining the Commodore most of his life was spent in the royal homes of England, and little did he think that he would go to sea assigned to England's top sea captain. He entered the Commodore's service in 1962 on the *Caronia,* when the then Captain Marr was taking the liner on a world cruise.

He confesses that he has never been a lover of the sea. "To be a seaman, I always maintain, one has to be born in the home of ships to have the calling of the sea. But I am very happy with the Commodore, and I hope to go until he retires. And when he retires, I shall retire from the sea and probably go back into a dusty old house again. At sea you can't read the London *Times* in the morning. I will look forward to when I can do that again.

"My duties ashore have given me the privilege of working in many reputable homes of England, one in particular being an appointment to the Royal Household of Buckingham Palace during the reign of King George V, and later with His Royal Highness the Duke of Gloucester at St. James Palace. During my term of duty with the Royals, I have held them in high respect, but always felt at ease.

"When in their company we were often addressed by our Christian names, whether attending a shooting party or official occasion. I felt I was a member of a great family."

Today, Hill likes to think of himself as a "butler at sea." His small but comfortable quarters are a few feet behind the Commodore's quarters high up in the forward structure of the *Elizabeth.* Here the valet is responsible for "the Commodore's household," which is sacred territory. As its keeper, Hill lives alone and apart from all the other members of the ship's crew.

"In this position," he explains, "one has to be prepared to live in remote surroundings; one would almost imagine the similarity of being the custodian of a great cathedral. It is not customary for anyone to enter the precincts unless on official business. All appointments must come through the Purser's office for passengers wishing to interview the Commodore or discuss any subject with him. When the visitors with proper permission arrive, it is then my duty to introduce them to the Commodore.

"Having been briefed by the Purser's office, and having studied the names of guests, I am expected, to the best of my ability, to remember their decorations and appointments in life and to be thoroughly conversant with their titles. Usually the guests of the Commodore range from dukes, duchesses, and archbishops to film stars and diplomats of almost every nation of the world."

That evening the main course of the special dinner which Hill served for the Commodore was beef Wellington—fillet of beef, cooked with cognac and truffles, then wrapped and baked in a delicate pastry crust. The meal concluded with crêpes Suzette prepared by Restaurant Manager Philp, who was dressed in tails and a high, stiff white wing collar. He worked at a portable table while Hill, the waiters, the Commodore's guests, and everyone in view watched with interest. Philp feels that the flaming French pancakes are still the most dramatic dish prepared and served in any dining room, and he works over the elegant dessert with the seriousness of a surgeon. As he concluded his preparations and blue flames rose from the brandy, waiters stepped forward for servings which Philp dished out one at a time.

Long after dessert the guests sat at the Captain's table talking and drinking coffee, though nearly everyone else had left the large dining salon. Hill, Philp, and their staffs waited in a row behind the table for the people to leave. Each remained stiffly at attention, carefully hiding any impatience that they might feel with the lingering guests. When the dining room was finally empty, the tables were quickly reset for the next day. Hill then went to the Commodore's quarters, which he found empty as expected. The steward could tell from the ship's motion that the storm was still very much alive, and he knew that the *Elizabeth*'s Master was on the bridge. Hill prepared for bed, though he didn't plan to turn in until Commodore Marr had returned and indicated he would not need his valet any more for the evening. It was after midnight when this happened. The worst of the storm was now behind the *Elizabeth,* and the Commodore, a very tired man, was ready for bed.

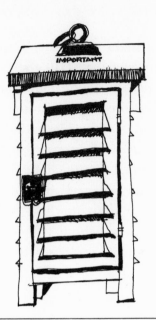

Chapter XIII

The Staff Captain
at Work

At dawn Friday, April 15, the *Queen Elizabeth* was beginning her second day of Voyage 424. She was steaming across a cold, comparatively smooth ocean, making a full 28½ knots. Nearly all the roll and pitch were gone. About 6:30 a.m. Chief Officer Arbuckle was pacing back and forth across the front of the wheelhouse. Each time that he turned and walked toward the liner's port side, the officer of the watch looked across the smooth gray sea over the port bow for something he expected to appear at any time. In a few minutes, he spotted what he was looking for, and called out: "Cape Race!" The sighting was noted in the *Elizabeth*'s log by Junior Second Officer Bennell. The snow-covered tip of Newfoundland's Avalon Peninsula appeared as a misty, white shape whose edges blended with the gray sea in the morning light.

The officers of the watch and their fellow crewmen on the bridge were undoubtedly the only ones to see Cape Race. The ship's clocks, for the second night, had been advanced an hour, and passengers accustomed to New York time were sleeping as though it were only 4:30 a.m. The beautiful liner glided silently by this northerly point of land from where she would soon stand on a great circle to Lands End.

That morning Commodore Marr remained in bed relatively late, for he badly needed to catch up on his rest. He had left a note asking Staff Captain Storey to check on the bridge before going down to breakfast, and the second in command fulfilled the request, arriving in the wheelhouse soon after 7:30. He looked over the charts and had a talk with Arbuckle. While they began by speaking of navigational problems, the subject was quickly changed to an unusual event that had occurred during the night. Upon arising, Captain Storey had read the night officer's report always left in the Staff Captain's quarters, and learned that a baby girl had been born just after midnight in the ship's hospital. The mother was Mrs. Janice Pentecost, a passenger on the way to England with her husband, Dr. Brian Pentecost, a cardiologist from Birmingham. The baby had arrived five weeks prematurely, but both mother and child were reported in good condition. "I assume the child will be named Elizabeth," said the officer of the watch, who already knew about the event. He was right.

This child was only the second or third born on the *Queen Elizabeth* in some three decades at sea, as far as anyone knows. Birth records for the ship have not been carefully preserved, but one other girl was born on the liner on December

3, 1946, as the ship approached the coast of England. The birth followed the vessel's passage through a heavy storm with 40-foot waves. The *Elizabeth*, which then had no fins, arrived home with twenty-two injured passengers—and a seven-pound baby girl christened "Elizabeth Dawn."

After his talk with Arbuckle, Captain Storey went down to the First Class Restaurant where he was one of only three eating so early. None of the seven assigned to his table near the center of the large salon were present; they had all announced that they would breakfast in their cabins throughout the voyage. The second in command, shaking his head, had stated that he would eat in the dining room every morning. "I never did like eating breakfast in my cabin," Captain Storey explained. "You have to take your food from one of those little tables with everything falling off while you're trying to balance it. I like to get up and get going. First of all, that requires a good breakfast down in the dining room."

While he ate a leisurely breakfast, with fried yellow perch as the entree, Captain Storey, who somehow maintains a well-trimmed waistline, wore black horn-rimmed glasses to read the radio dispatches. He first read news dispatches some of which would appear in the ship's daily newspaper, the *Ocean Times*. It is published along with menus, entertainment programs, and scores of other items in the *Elizabeth*'s busy print shop. He concluded his reading with a sheaf of radio dispatches concerning the ship's business. When he finished eating, the second in command gathered up his papers and headed back to his quarters next to the Commodore's.

In a few minutes, there was a knock on his door. A half dozen men entered led by the *Elizabeth*'s Chief Master at Arms and her Day Officer who is the Staff Captain's right-hand man. With them were the liner's "hygiene man" responsible for the ship's sanitary condition, especially the elimination of "livestock" (bugs and vermin which are bound to find their way aboard any large steamship). The group also included the ship's joiner and a couple of his staff. In the next 20 minutes the group talked about matters concerning the ship's operation. When the business was through the men promptly left Captain Storey's quarters.

This was the usual beginning of a day of meetings for the *Elizabeth*'s second in command, who, at fifty-three, has been going to sea nearly forty years. Every day at sea, Captain Storey moved from one meeting to the next, between which were sandwiched inspections, paperwork, special ceremonies, and a dozen other duties spelled out in the Cunard book of rules. When not working, the Staff Captain, like the one man senior to him, conducts his personal table in the dining room with a selected list of guests. Afterwards, however, he may or may not relax with his guests in the lounge, for there can be more meetings with crewmen concerning the proper internal operation of the *Queen Elizabeth*.

Captain Storey, according to the Cunard rules, is responsible for the "smooth working of all departments on board to maintain their efficiency for the safety, comfort, and general well-being of the passengers." The job is comparable to the combined duties of several officials in a small city. The Staff Captain, for example, acts as the judge aboard the *Queen Elizabeth,* and he is required to sit nearly every day. Promptly at 11 a.m. in his quarters, Captain Storey deals with "defaulters," which, most of the time, means crewmen who have misbehaved. Perhaps they have failed to report to their watches on time, or they have been rude to passengers or superiors. The guilty defaulter is often fined by a loss of pay, and in serious cases, he may be incarcerated in a cabin for the remainder of the voyage. It's unlikely that the Staff Captain would sit in judgment of a passenger, but it could happen in case of a crime at sea. The accused would be turned over to civil authorities in the country of his nationality, if possible, or if not in the next port.

Captain Storey frequently corrects a landlubber's common misconception that a ship's captain or staff captain can perform the legal rites of matrimony. "That isn't true on a British ship," he explains, "and I know of no other national ship registry where it would be true. Of course, there no doubt have been sea captains who have wrongly assumed they could marry people. I can understand how that might result in a lot of people thinking they are legally married when they are not."

Besides acting as the *Queen Elizabeth*'s municipal judge the Staff Captain is also her health officer, an important and endless job. "Apart from the ordinary problems of keeping conditions sanitary anywhere," explains Captain Storey, "there are always additional difficulties on a passenger liner simply because you are confined. Furthermore, you are very much exposed to some trying sanitary problems. It's difficult, for example, to remain free of insect life. They have the same problem in the best hotels. You have a ship like this starting from New York with two thousand passengers and another thousand or more crew, it's hard to imagine that all these people will come aboard without bringing something with them. They do. And also, in any port where you store, things come on board in the stores. It's a constant battle all the time, but it's a battle that we are always winning. We have to."

Many of the Staff Captain's multiple responsibilities are the product of century-old maritime traditions, as when a death on board leads to burial at sea. There was a case in point on the *Queen Elizabeth*'s eastbound crossing of Voyage 425. A night steward who had been going to sea for more than three decades was found dead at his post. When Captain Storey learned of his death, he promptly consulted the ship's head doctor because disposal of human remains is first determined from a medical point of view. Will keeping the body aboard endanger passengers and crew? In this case the doctor answered negatively, but when Captain Storey radioed the next of kin in England, word came back that the deceased had desired to be buried at sea, and the family would like the wish fulfilled. The Staff Captain immediately took steps to inter the body in a watery grave. He first carried a bottle of rum to the *Elizabeth*'s boatswain in advance payment for wrapping the body in canvas, loading the shroud with enough weight for it to sink, and finally sewing it up. The boatswain completed the sewing job by drawing the last stitch through the dead man's nose, a final act carried over from doctorless days to ascertain that the deceased had truly passed from this world before leaving him to the sea.

"Now I have never learned," says Captain Storey, "if the rum is to be given to the boatswain in payment before or after the job is done. But I being of an understanding nature give it to him before he starts the gruesome task and needs the rum."

At 8 a.m. of the day following the boatswain's duties to the dead, nearly three hundred crewmen stood silently in mourning at the stern on the *Queen Elizabeth*'s mooring deck. The shrouded body was covered with a Union Jack and wreaths of flowers fashioned by the ship's gardener (florist). It rested on a board balanced on the outer rail by seamen dressed in their British Merchant Marine uniforms. The religious ceremony was conducted by one of the ship's doctors who is also an ordained minister, and as he read from Genesis 3:19, ". . . for dust thou art and unto dust shalt thou return," the seamen tilted the board and the body slid from under the Union Jack. It dropped over 30 feet into the Atlantic and disappeared as the great liner steamed toward Europe.

"At that point it is very important for the body to sink because it is extremely bad luck should it remain afloat," explains Captain Storey, whose education in life at sea goes back to his earliest training on H.M.S. *Conway,* an aged British battleship sometimes compared to the American *Constitution.*

On Voyage 424 there fortunately were no deaths aboard the *Elizabeth*—indeed the passenger list was increased by one because of the birth that April 15. Captain Storey, after his morning round of meetings and inspections, paid a visit to the liner's small but remarkably complete hospital to learn that the mother and child were doing very well.

He then took a stroll alone up through the liner to the Verandah Grill where the chef had been having trouble with one of the cooking ranges. The chef explained the problem and assured the Staff Captain that the repairs had been made and the range could now operate with complete safety.

From there Captain Storey returned to his quarters, prepared for lunch, and telephoned the Day Officer to say that he could be found for the next hour or two at his table in the dining room. Shortly after 1 p.m. he joined his table guests whose company he enjoyed through a leisurely lunch. Captain Storey has commanded most of Cunard's cargo ships, but he prefers life on the company's passenger liners, many of which he has also commanded. He likes people and states that he has never arrived in port glad to be free of any of the thousands of passengers he met. He says: "If you didn't enjoy life on the liners, you would pack up and say, 'Keep me in cargo where the cargo doesn't talk back.' "

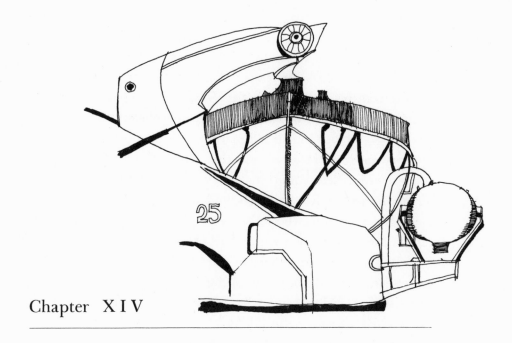

25

Chapter X I V

On the
Grand Banks

As Captain Storey finished his morning's work and was going
to lunch, the *Queen Elizabeth* was crossing one of the world's
most interesting stretches of ocean. From Cape Race she had
continued slightly to the northeast out across the famous
Grand Banks, formed by the tops of a submerged mountain
range some 300 miles long and 80 to 100 fathoms deep. The
Banks, famous for cod, herring, mackerel, and flounder har-
vested by fishing vessels from all around the Atlantic, have
long played a role in trans-Atlantic travel. They bisect the

great-circle route from northern Europe to Canadian and United States ports. As trans-Atlantic travel grew in the nineteenth century, traffic over the Banks became so heavy that they were the scene of many mid-ocean collisions. The danger became so serious that it led in 1885 to a proposal for east and west steamship tracks across the area. The suggestion was made by Matthew Fontaine Maury in his "Sailing Directions" where he called for an eastbound lane to pass just south of Cape Race and a westbound lane to proceed over the southern end of the area, known as the Tail of the Banks.

But the greatest danger of the Grand Banks turned out to be sea ice, especially icebergs and growlers (small masses of ice but still navigational hazards), carried southward by the Labrador Current across the Banks to the Tail of the Banks. The amount of ice varies widely from year to year. In 1929, for example, there were nearly 1,300 icebergs sighted on the Banks below the 48th parallel, while in 1940, 1958, and 1963 only a few were seen. The most famous iceberg disaster, the sinking of the *Titanic,* occurred just south of the Tail of the Banks in 1912. The disaster's world-wide publicity generated the pressure that led to the 1913 International Convention for the Safety of Life at Sea. Out of this came the now famous International Ice Patrol sponsored by several nations and still operated by the United States Coast Guard. Today's Ice Patrol, using special vessels and planes, continually surveys the Grand Banks, reporting any ice conditions. In New York, the officers of the *Queen Elizabeth* had picked up the Patrol's latest ice reports through the local branch of the Oceanographic Office. Then, as they proceeded on Voyage 424, the *Elizabeth*'s radio room received two ice broadcasts daily from stations in Washington, D.C., and Halifax, Nova Scotia. The reports indicated that the northern route which Commodore Marr eventually chose was free of any dangerous ice.

Compounding the dangers of ice on the Grand Banks is the heavy fog which has plagued mariners for centuries. In his *Natural History of North America,* Nicholas Denys reported in 1672 that, "The Grand Bank is rarely without mist or fog, which is sometimes so thick that one cannot see from one end of the ship to the other." The blame is laid upon the cold Labrador Current mixing with the warm Gulf Stream along a line called the "cold wall," which, in spring and early summer, parallels the south and southeastern edges of the Grand Banks. When the cold waters of the Labrador Current meet the warm, moist air of the Gulf Stream, the result is fog which blankets the ocean on the inner side of the cold wall.

The Ice Patrol and today's radar make the Banks much less dangerous than in the past, but it is still no place for laxity. In fact, the Cunard Steam-Ship Company orders its masters to stay off the Banks. The exception to the rule, of course, is the ancient and unquestioned prerogative of a ship's master to take whatever action he considers best for the safety of his vessel and her passengers. Commodore Marr's choice of a course over the Banks was an exercise of that right as he avoided one of the roughest storms of a decade. Besides there being no dangerous ice reported, the Banks would be completely traversed in the light of a day which held good promise of fog-free visibility.

All Friday morning, April 15, the *Queen Elizabeth*'s depth recorder indicated she was steaming over the Banks in water less than 100 fathoms deep. This would remain the case until she would leave the Banks, when the depth would drop quickly to thousands of fathoms. Late in the morning, the liner began encountering mist which hung in patches over the fairly calm water. The worst of these areas of gray, wet air cut the visibility intermittently, but not seriously. The sun which had been hidden since the liner's arrival in New York was still

hidden by a solid layer of clouds. It was not too cold outside—
between 30 and 40 degrees—and the atmosphere was dank. It
seemed heavy enough to dampen sound, yet the endless howl
of wind on the bridge continued, though more subdued than
during the worst of the storm.

Although the officers and men in the wheelhouse appeared outwardly calm, there was a tangible increase in tension for they had been officially informed that they now had to
be especially alert. As the patches of mist appeared ahead,
Commodore Marr ordered a slight reduction in propeller revolutions, bringing the *Elizabeth*'s speed down somewhat
below the 28½ knots called for by the schedule. Simultaneously he called out the order: "Stand by!" whereupon the
liner's telegraphs were pulled back from the "Full Ahead"
position and placed on the "Stand By" position. With the
order, the engineering crew on duty was increased, and the
men moved to special engine-room stations from which they
could take immediate action to stop the ship as quickly as
possible should an emergency demand it.

The speed reduction and the "stand by" order were
super-precautionary measures taken by the Commodore, in
consideration of the unusual course he had been forced to
take. Actually, steaming through such patches of mist, particularly with the *Elizabeth*'s sophisticated radar, could be considered as safe as sailing on a completely clear day. Even the
smallest fishing boats, which might be hard to pick out with
the naked eye, are revealed by the radar. Incidentally, many
fishing boats, to insure that they will appear on the screens,
mount special metal reflectors on their mastheads to bounce
radar waves back to where they come from.

"I may not be able to go down to dinner again this evening," said Commodore Marr after he had put his liner on
"Stand By."

"Oh, we should be out of this long before dinner, sir," said Junior First Officer Finlay, who was on watch.

The Commodore slid open the starboard door to the wheelhouse and walked out onto the flying bridge. About the only wind now came from the ship's forward movement, a mild breeze compared to what had hit the liner during the past twenty-four hours. The ship's Master looked down over the outer rail at the ocean sweeping by more than 90 feet below. Here was the kind of sea that could make a steamship captain's life a dream. "Mist and fog are portrayed as one of our greatest problems," explains Commodore Marr, "but actually it offers a sea with some of the best steaming possible. The wind is low; the sea is calm. Our laws, however, still keep us from taking advantage of such conditions, although modern radar and other navigational aids could make it safe."

International maritime law still maintains that vessels in fog must proceed at a "moderate" speed at which the ship can be stopped within the distance of visibility. For a large liner such as the *Queen Elizabeth*, this means bringing her almost to a stop when she encounters a heavy fog. With her great length, a dense fog could even prevent the *Elizabeth*'s officers from seeing her bow. Captains of large liners have measured fogs with sort of a "funnel index." Looking back from the flying bridge, they count how many funnels are visible as an index to a fog's density. "The *Queen Elizabeth*'s two funnels don't give you enough to work with," says Commodore Marr. "Older liners had more. The *Mary* has three. The old *Mauritania* and *Aquitania* each had four."

Returning to the wheelhouse, the Commodore spent a few minutes observing the radar, which was continuously under surveillance by a trained seaman. On the Grand Banks, the screen almost always indicated the presence of at least one other vessel. At the moment a single spot of light represented a vessel off the *Elizabeth*'s starboard bow. The course of this boat, some 15 miles away, was being plotted, and she was obviously taking a zigzag course which would not bring her near the *Elizabeth*.

"He's trawling over the Banks," commented Commodore Marr. "Probably a Portuguese boat. There seem to be a lot of them along about here."

For the next few hours, as the giant liner continued through the misty conditions, the Commodore devoted most of his time to reviewing the ship's long-range navigation for Voyage 424. Late weather data had just been applied to a chart that portrayed the Atlantic's current pressure patterns. The Commodore was now particularly interested in the large low-pressure system that had been causing serious storm conditions from Iceland to the Azores and had been responsible for damaging the *Michelangelo*. This low was still between the *Elizabeth* and Cherbourg, and its status was of considerable concern to the liner's master. He had ducked the worst of one great storm, but knew it would be impossible to go around this second system if it were still intact as he approached Europe.

"She is beginning to fill, and that is very good," said the Commodore, after a quick glance at the new chart. He meant that the storm was starting to weaken. The newly drawn isobars told him so because they were farther apart than on the previous chart, which he held to one side for comparison. The difference in isobar spacing was enough for the Commodore to conclude that he was definitely through dodging low-pressure patterns.

At 3:25 p.m., the *Queen Elizabeth* was at 47 degrees and 59 minutes north in latitude and 47 degrees 32 minutes west in longitude, and she stood on a 70-degree heading. This placed her on Track "F," which ends at Bishop Rock on the

Scilly Isles, southwest of England's famous Lands End. The master of a liner heading for Bishop Rock actually plans to pass two and a third miles south of the Rock, which is famous in the annals of trans-Atlantic travel because a crossing from Europe to New York is often defined by mariners as "from Bishop Rock to Ambrose."

To place the liner on Track "F," her officers first plotted a great circle from a point just off Cape Race to the spot in the ocean a bit south of Bishop Rock. Being an eastbound vessel, she was then held to a course ten miles south and parallel to the great circle. Westbound ships on Track "F" always remain ten miles north of the line. For the Europe-bound *Elizabeth*, the overall course would take her northeast until she passed the meridian of 30 degrees west where she would come around to the east and then slowly turn southeast toward Bishop Rock. This route was laid out in a light pencil line on the liner's main navigational chart in the wheelhouse.

While the ship was still passing through the mist, Commodore Marr used this course line to determine how well he was holding to schedule. He spread the points of a pair of dividers a distance that on the scale of the chart represented one good day's run of the *Queen Elizabeth*. "We're here now," said the ship's Master, placing one of the two needle points on the liner's current position, "and tomorrow this time we'll be here." He brought the second divider point to rest along the vessel's planned route at a spot near the meridian of 30 degrees west and a bit above the parallel of 50 degrees north. Holding this second point in place, he whirled the first divider arm until its point touched another position on the ship's planned course. "And on Sunday at this time we'll be here," said the Commodore, referring to a position not far from the southern coast of Ireland. Another whirl placed the easternmost divider point well beyond the coast of France, and the Commodore knew right then that the *Queen Eliza-beth*—the weather, the Lord, and all else permitting—could arrive at Cherbourg on time Monday morning. In fact, with a little luck, he could even come into the French port with time to spare; or better, he might reduce propeller revolutions on the last day of the voyage, save some fuel, and still arrive on time.

The Commodore was obviously pleased. He had not only avoided a major storm, but he had done very well with his schedule. Had he held to the originally planned course on Track "B" he might not only have endangered the *Queen Elizabeth* and the souls aboard, but the rough storm might also have forced him to slow down. He might even have had to stop completely with his prow pointed into the wind to wait for better weather.

"It is likely now," said the *Elizabeth*'s Master, "that we will encounter some very fine weather before we arrive. We will probably run through heavy swells before we get in, and they may cause some more pitching in the next twenty-four hours, but I think we're leaving most of our troubles." The swells would come as an aftermath of the storm on the eastern Atlantic; inertia would maintain the powerful waves well after the atmospheric disturbance had disappeared.

By late afternoon, the British liner was off the Grand Banks and passing the cold wall into the warmer waters of the North Atlantic Current (which is the name of the Gulf Stream system after it passes the Tail of the Banks). She was breaking out of the mist which had threatened but never seriously hampered the visibility, for more than half the day. The Commodore decided that favorable steaming this evening would permit him to join the passengers. It was definitely time, he thought, to pay more attention to the social side of his profession. He left the bridge shortly after 5 p.m. and went to his quarters to take a quick nap before several passengers came for cocktails around 7 p.m. Before going to his bedroom the Commodore telephoned the *Elizabeth*'s Purser, Fergus Pritchard, to say that finally the weather was going to cooperate in making the remainder of Voyage 424 a smoother ride. Because good steaming usually means that the passengers enjoy themselves more, the Purser's people are busier, as they are responsible for the entertainment.

Chapter XV

Pleasures of Passage

"The fastest way of getting from A to B today is by jet airplane," says Fergus Pritchard, the *Elizabeth*'s Purser, who came with Cunard in the 1920's rather than pursue his intended career as an actor. "Going by sea is now more of a holiday concept. Much, much more entertainment is required than previously. Relaxation is as important as getting to one's destination—and in many cases, much more important."

The responsibility for a "holiday concept" aboard the *Queen* Ships falls to the Purser's department. Traditionally he is the clerk of a passenger vessel who keeps the ship's accounts and serves as paymaster for the crew. This is still an important part of Pritchard's responsibilities, but it is now one of two divisions overseered by the Purser. Under him are two assistant pursers, one responsible for the ship's clerical needs, the other for her entertainment.

"I sometimes picture myself as the general manager of a big hotel," explains Pritchard. "There you would find yourself in charge of accounts, entertainment, and a host of other responsibilities. Well, it works that way here on the *Elizabeth*.

"Altogether today's job of purser on a ship like either of the *Queens* is a big job. When we have a full load of passengers, we'll do business amounting to hundreds of thousands of dollars. We have a dozen bars that bring in a lot of money. Then there are the many shops around the ship, and we're responsible for their accounting. It's really like a small town afloat. The town even has a bank—the Midland Bank has a branch right on the *Elizabeth*. In England they have about 2,500 branches and we have one of them.

"But it is more than a small town afloat. The people are really not as they would be at home. They're naturally travelers, and many are on holiday. So they create special problems, of course. For example, take the matter of postage stamps. We use a lot of them on board, and they have to come from the different countries we visit. The problem of carrying many different stamps is especially complicated on a cruise where you're visiting many countries. We have to plan ahead and have enough stamps on hand so that people can mail their letters and postal cards with the proper stamps in all the countries we visit."

OVERLEAF:

This bulletin of notices and entertainment was distributed on Voyage 424 to first-class passengers the day after departure from New York.

NOTICES

MEETING POINTS

At 11.45 a.m. — For the "Under - 12's"
A "Coketail" Party in the Starboard Side Garden Lounge
At 9.30 p.m. — For the "Teens" & "Twenties" — A Get-Together
in the Cavern, Main Deck Aft.

CHERBOURG DISEMBARKATION & TRAIN ARRANGEMENTS

Passengers disembarking at Cherbourg are requested to call at the Travel Bureau on Prom. Deck today between 9.00 a.m. and Noon or from 2.00 to 5.00 p.m. to complete their disembarkation arrangements and also to make their Boat Train reservations and purchase rail tickets to Paris.

ARRIVAL SOUTHAMPTON

Train leaves Southampton at 9.00 a.m. — due Waterloo 10.54 a.m. Tuesday, April 19th

Passengers who wish to travel on the Boat Train to London are kindly requested to make their train reservations and purchase their train tickets at the Purser's Office on 'A' Deck as soon as convenient.

It is important that reservations for both the Cherbourg and the Southampton Boat Trains are made as early in the voyage as possible in order that we may radio ahead for the necessary accommodation.

ENTERTAINMENT

Swimming Pools
From 7.00 a.m. to 7.00 p.m.

Squash Court (Sun Deck) Hours:
From 7.00 a.m. to 1.00 p.m. and from 2.00 to 7.00 p.m.
The attendant may be located in the Squash Court or in the Gymnasium. Instruction available from 10.00 a.m. to 1.00 p.m.

Gymnasium Hours:
Men: 7.00 to 9.00 a.m.   Children: 9.00 to 10.00 a.m.
Ladies: 10.00 to 11.00 a.m.
Mixed: 2.00 to 3.30 p.m. and 5.30 to 7.00 p.m.

Turkish Baths:
Ladies: 10.00 a.m. - 2.00 p.m.
Men: 7.00 a.m. - 9.30 a.m. and 2.30 p.m. - 7.00 p.m.

a.m.
7.30—"General Knowledge" Competition (delivered to staterooms)

10.00—Ladies' Keep-Fit Class   Gymnasium

10.45—Ray Baines at the Organ   "Queen Elizabeth" Lounge

11.30—Totalisator on the Ship's Run   Prom. Deck Square
        Can you guess how many miles the ship has covered
        from noon yesterday until noon today?
        Winners paid shortly after noon or at the Purser's Bureau

Noon - 1.00 p.m.—Cocktail Music   Midships Bar
              with the Dougie Ward Trio

2.30—Bridge Tournament   **Smoke Room**
        Play commences at 2.30 p.m. and finishes at 4.30 p.m. Miss Frances Milroy, Social Directress, will be in attendance to effect introductions and arrange tables.

2.30—Recorded Concert   Midships Bar
        Symphony No. 6 in F Major (Op. 68) "Pastoral" *Beethoven*
        The Vienna Philharmonic Orchestra
        Conductor: Wilhelm Furtwängler

2.45—Table Tennis Tournament   Promenade Deck
        (Competitors to meet at tables)

3.45—Marcel Torrent and the String Orchestra present
        Music for Tea-Time in the Main Lounge

6.00—"The Voice of America" News Broadcast   Midships Bar

6.15—B.B.C. News Broadcast   Midships Bar

7.30 (from)—Dinner served   Mid-Ocean Restaurant

9.00—Orchestral Selections   "Queen Elizabeth" Lounge
        Marcel Torrent and the String Orchestra

9.45—Horse Racing and Bingo   "Queen Elizabeth" Lounge
             followed by
           CABARET DANCE
         featuring at 11 00 p.m.
          Felipe and Olga

             ★

       George Cormack and Irene Sharp

Midnight—Verandah Grill Opens — Ray Baines at the Piano

12.30 (unaltered time)—DANCING   Verandah Grill
          The Jimmy Watson Quintet

TODAY'S MOVIE PROGRAMME

Showing at 4.30 and 9.30 p.m.

"Heroes of Telemark"
Featuring Kirk Douglas, Richard Harris and Ulla Jacobson
(Showing time: 2 hours, 11 minutes)

CLOCKS
Clocks will be ADVANCED ONE HOUR at MIDNIGHT

Entertainment is, however, the most important part of the Purser's job today, for people in their week or so at sea want to be entertained. With all the passengers on a *Queen*, many different kinds of entertainment are in demand. Nearly all want movies, so the *Elizabeth* has two theaters, one for first and cabin classes, one for tourist class. There is a different movie each day of a voyage. Some passengers expect live entertainment: dancers, singers, and nightclub entertainers. Others want to be stimulated intellectually. They may expect lectures or the opportunity to learn a foreign language, or at least brush up on one. But a lot of passengers want no entertainment at all, but to be left alone, and the pursers must make certain there's an opportunity for that.

"One thing about the *Queen Elizabeth*," says Pritchard, "we've got room to accommodate all kinds of tastes. And if a person wants to be left alone we have all kinds of space to satisfy him."

On the Friday during Voyage 424 the *Queen Elizabeth*'s entertainment program offered an extensive list of things to do. Her two movie theaters had three showings of an up-to-the-minute Kirk Douglas drama. There were several concerts, both live and recorded. At 10:30 a.m. first-class passengers were offered an organ concert in the main lounge by organist Ray Baines. A musical trio played for passengers before lunch and at the evening cocktail hour. At 3:45 p.m. passengers at tea listened to Marcel Torrent and his string orchestra. All day people could play games of many varieties, enter bridge tournaments and table tennis matches, or take a workout in the ship's well-equipped gymnasiums. Each day the passengers played "Totalizator on the Ship's Run," in which a money pool was won by the individual who came closest in guessing how many miles the ship sailed from noon to noon.

After dinner that evening, Commodore Marr and his table guests went to the main lounge which was packed with passengers and the ship's top officers. As the Commodore's group arrived, people were playing bingo, which alternates with the traditional wooden horse racing game as an early evening diversion on the ocean liner. When the game was over, the center floor was cleared, and people danced to Marcel Torrent's orchestra. An hour later the dancing was interrupted for a parade of the entrants in a crazy-hat contest before a panel of judges. Some of the entrants, all female passengers, had worked the entire day on the headpieces. One lady, who was awarded a prize for "originality," wore a patch over one eye, the replica of a half grapefruit on her head, and a sign around her neck, reading "A little squirt." Commodore Marr, when called forward to present the prizes, was somewhat embarrassed, but he courageously carried out the assignment with poise.

At 11 p.m. the evening's cabaret entertainment featured a group of six English pop singers, in the style of the famous Beatles. The young singers, "The Applejacks," had become the ship's most popular entertainers. They had already appeared in cabin and tourist class and gained many admirers who followed them into first class, though passengers are asked to remain within their own classes aboard the *Elizabeth*. The Applejacks' wild, animated, and highly amplified singing with many loud and unusual discords stood in sharp contrast to the ship's subdued string orchestra and, indeed, to the conservative, darkly paneled room itself. The five young men (one of whom looked like a young Abraham Lincoln) and a girl evoked many different reactions from the passengers. One of the Commodore's guests felt the Applejacks were the best entertainers he had heard aboard any ship, and one lady said the Commodore should give the order to "Throw them overboard!"

At midnight Commodore Marr and a few of his most durable guests went to the Verandah Grill, which reopens

with a small orchestra at 12 o'clock for first-class passengers who care for a late supper and more dancing. The Commodore had a sandwich and a glass of milk and left to go to
bed.

Before turning in for the night, he walked forward to the
bridge where he talked with the officer of the watch, Junior
First Officer Finlay, to learn that all was in good order. The
Elizabeth was meeting some of the long rolling swells that her
Master had expected, but she was not pitching too badly. The
bow was rising slowly, quietly, and gently, then dipping
firmly but gracefully into the ice-cold waters of the North
Atlantic. She was nearing 40 degrees west in longitude, south
of Greenland's east coast.

Commodore Marr, deciding to take a breath of the sea
air, stepped outside on the starboard flying bridge where the
weather was pleasant, though the liner had just run through a
line of rain squalls. The sea was dark all around, but breaks in
the cloud cover revealed patches of sky brilliant with stars. He
walked to the wing from where he could look back across the
starboard side of the huge steamship he commanded. On the
sea far below, flecks of light from the *Elizabeth*'s hundreds of
portholes sparkled on the water. The drama—the expanses of
ocean, clouds, and sky dwarfing the great liner with funnels
the size of castles pushing through the North Atlantic's night
air—stirred the Commodore, as had similar scenes a thousand
times before. For a few moments he remained on his bridge
taking in the dramatic picture, which brought to mind some
verses of a poem by Rudyard Kipling, "The Secret of the
Machines," one of many he had memorized as a young officer
on long night watches at sea.

> *Would you call a friend from half across the world?*
> *If you'll let us have his name and town and state,*
> *You shall see and hear your crackling question hurled*

As seen from the main deck just aft of the knighthead, the Queen Elizabeth *steams under the Verrazano-Narrows Bridge as she approaches New York's Upper Bay. The large chain in the left foreground is attached to the anchor which drops from near the top of her sharply raked prow. Two other anchor chains, controlling anchors at each side of the bow, are seen on each side. The chains, each 900 feet long, weigh a total of 225 tons. One link is two feet long.*

The Sandy Hook pilot boards the Queen Elizabeth *from his motor launch by climbing a ladder and entering a shell door on the liner's port side.*

As the Coast Guard Cutter Manitou
approaches the Elizabeth's *starboard beam
to deliver Cunard and U.S. government
officials, the Day Officer and a crewman
wait to assist the boarding party. The*
Manitou *is being watched by ship's
officers on the flying bridge,
projecting over the liner's side
forward and 90 feet above the water.*

The Queen Elizabeth *steams along
Ambrose Channel as she completes he[r]
423rd voyage as a grand hotel of the
North Atlantic.*

*Geoffrey Thrippleton Marr, Commodore of the Cunard Fleet
and Captain of the* Queen Elizabeth, *on the flying bridge of
his liner as she proceeds up the Hudson River.*

The Queen Elizabeth *moves slowly up the Hudson River with Manhattan in the background. Four tugs are secured to the liner as they make ready for the docking pilot to swing her abreast of the river and move the liner into Pier 92. The other large ship docked in the background is the S.S. United States.*

As the **Elizabeth** *is being docked at New York's Pier 92, directly ahead, three tugs on her starboard bow act as a pivot to hold the bow while the stern is swung up the river at low-water slack.*

Captain Thomas Port, the Sandy Hook pilot, watches from the wheelhouse as he calls out headings that will take the liner on a safe course through the busy traffic of New York Harbor.

Commodore G. T. Marr, Reynolds Pilot Grover A. Sanschagrin, and Junior First Officer John Finlay (l. to r.) on the Elizabeth's *port wing a few moments before undocking for departure on Voyage 424. A red line on the outer rail of the flying bridge must be exactly opposite the center of the* Elizabeth's *sign for her to be properly docked, with her doors on the post side aligned with gangways. Commodore Marr is watching the removal of gangways before ordering the liner to leave the pier. Captain Sanschagrin is the docking pilot who will guide the steamship out into the Hudson and then turn her over to a Sandy Hook pilot to take the liner out to sea.*

As the Elizabeth *begins to move astern, leaving her New York pier, seamen
tie down the rigging on the forward mast. Manhattan's elevated West Side
Highway is seen just beyond the liner's bow.*

This device, called a clear-view screen, serves in effect as a windshield wiper for the wheelhouse windows. There are two of these screens on the Elizabeth's bridge. The electric motor at the top whirls a circular plate of glass enclosed within the ring. Rain or spray striking the wheelhouse windows will not collect on the whirling glass.

The Elizabeth's prow cuts through a large wave during the storm encountered on Voyage 424. Spray from such waves was often thrown over the wheelhouse, from which this picture was taken.

Navigating officer works over a special Decca chart of the North Atlantic.
Decca Navigator (device with three dials behind lamp) receives and
electronically analyzes radio signals from groups of land-based Decca
broadcasting stations. Information then appears on the machine's dials
and enables the navigator to plot the ship's position.

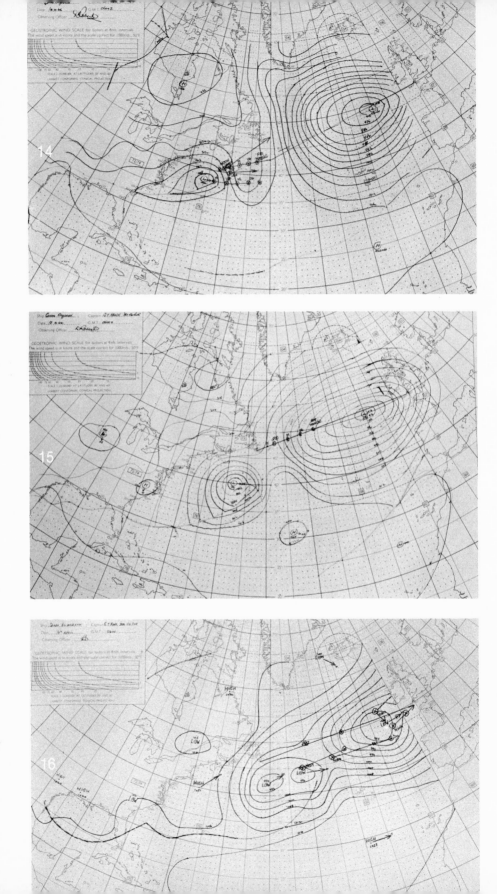

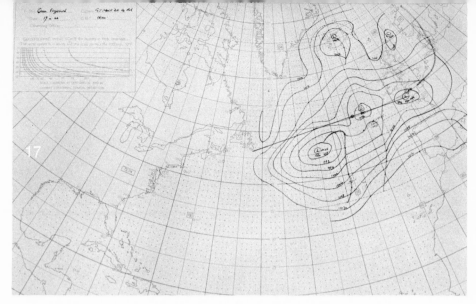

Four North Atlantic weather charts used on the Elizabeth's Voyage 424
from April 14 to 17, 1966 (numbered tabs indicate dates). The
large pattern of concentric circles to the right on the 14th represents one of
the worst Atlantic storms of many years. The concentric circles in the
western Atlantic represent the smaller but still very rough storm
that tested Commodore Marr's navigational skills as he swung the liner
around the pattern to the north. The long straight lines running
diagonally across the charts indicate the liner's route.

Commodore Marr (r.)
working over the Elizabeth's
main navigation chart in the
wheelhouse as the liner
proceeds over the North
Atlantic on Voyage 424.
Behind him are his two
watch officers. The
quartermaster who is
steering the ship is to
the left out of sight.
Two of the liner's four
telegraphs are shown at
the picture's left; they
are connected with the
two engine rooms.

One of the Queen Elizabeth's *two well-wiped engine rooms. Each room contains two of the ship's four propelling machinery units. A unit consists of four turbines grouped around a main gear wheel and coupled with one of the liner's four great propeller shafts. The two turbines shown here are run by superheated steam at 750° F. and 425 pounds per square inch pressure.*

The Queen Elizabeth's main control office for its radiotelegraph and radiotelephone service, which reaches all over the world. Transmitters located in other parts of the ship are controlled from this office. All first-class accommodations on the Elizabeth have bedside telephones with which passengers can reach anywhere in the world via the liner's radio office. The office also handles all official ship's communications.

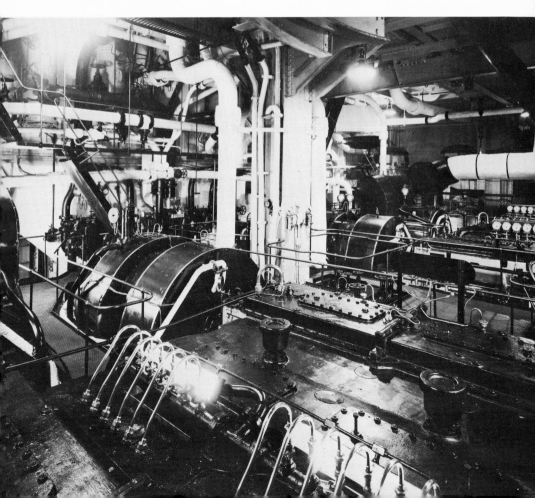

The Queen Elizabeth, *her 1,031 feet of length foreshortened by the long lens of a flying cameraman, is shown running full ahead at sea not far from Nantucket Island.*

Late on a sunny afternoon in mid-Atlantic, Junior Second Officer A. C.
Bennell uses his personal sextant to shoot the sun for navigational
purposes. He is standing on the flying bridge on the port side. In the
upper right are two radar antennas mounted on the wheelhouse roof;
the larger one belongs to the ship's main radar set. When in operation
the antennas slowly whirl, scanning the ocean all about the liner.

A quartermaster on the Elizabeth's starboard wing uses a telescope to watch
the Cherbourg tugs at the stern of the long liner. Lines are being
thrown to the tugs, and when they are made fast, the quartermaster will
announce the fact to the Cherbourg pilot and ship's officers on the bridge.

Chief Quartermaster Charles Ernest Bell, at the Elizabeth's *main wheel, steers into Cherbourg under the direction of the port's harbor pilot, Captain Jean Burel (right). The officer next to Captain Burel is Junior First Officer John Finlay; two other quartermasters and a messenger are to the rear. To Bell's right is the ship's auxiliary wheel. A third steering wheel, to the right, is part of the ship's automatic pilot. The ship's compass is contained in the large, shiny housing or binnacle in front of Bell. The flared tubes above Bell are designed for voice communication about the bridge, but have seldom been used in the ship's latter days. The two gauges labeled "Ford" and "Aft," on the wall in the background, indicate the revolutions of the forward and after starboard propellers.*

Workmen on the quay at Cherbourg haul in the first line from the
Queen Elizabeth *as she docks toward the end of Voyage 424.*

The Queen Elizabeth *takes on stores in Southampton. Bags
of potatoes are being loaded over an escalator.*

Once a year all during her life, the Elizabeth
*has been drydocked in Southampton for a major
overhaul, which includes cleaning and
inspecting all underwater parts. The man at
work scraping barnacles was photographed
just after the ship's final World War II
military service and before her official
maiden voyage in 1946. Behind and above
"Barnacle Bill" are two workmen inspecting
the liner's after starboard propeller. During
another drydocking pictured here, workmen are
cleaning and inspecting one of the* Elizabeth's
*great anchor chains. One of her three 16-ton
anchors is at the rear left.*

Well-known English witch Sybil Leek defies superstition as she sails in the superliner **QUEEN ELIZABETH**.

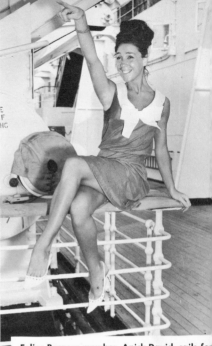

Folies Bergère member, Anick David, sails for in the **QUEEN ELIZABETH**.

The sailing or arrival of a Cunard Queen liner has always been the occasion for publicity pictures. These are samples from hundreds of such photographs offered over the years by the Cunard publicity office in New York.

Lord Montagu of Beaulieu, England arrives in the **QUEEN ELIZABETH** with his famed 1909 Silver Ghost Rolls Royce.

In 1966 the Queen Elizabeth *was returned to her builder on the Clyde in Scotland and the ship underwent a major renovation costing some $4 million. She was completely air-conditioned, and a new lido deck with an outdoor swimming pool was added to the stern, as shown in this photograph taken right after the work was completed.*

*These photographs, taken by the John Brown and
Company Ltd. at Clydebank, Scotland, in 1936 and 1937,
show the* Queen Elizabeth *in the early building
stages. Her keel was laid (above) in December 1936.
The construction of the 40,000-ton hull took
3,000 workmen almost two years.*

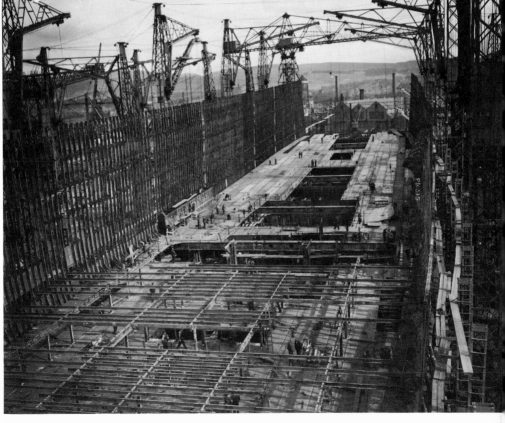

On September 27, 1938, only three days before completion of the
Munich Pact, the Queen Elizabeth was launched. Queen Elizabeth (now
the Queen Mother), with her daughters Princess Elizabeth and
Princess Margaret, christened the ship.

The beautiful hull of the new Queen Elizabeth *in her building site on the Clyde just before launching in 1938.*

In February 1940 the great new liner was painted gray, and tugs hauled her from the fitting-out basin where workmen had nearly completed the ship after the launch in 1938. She was vulnerable to German bombs, and the fitting-out basin was needed for work on warships. The gray Elizabeth *is shown here quietly leaving the Clyde for her secret voyage to New York.*

After her secret voyage to New York in 1940 the Elizabeth (foreground) was tied up with her sister ship, the Mary (opposite side of the same pier). The third large liner is the Normandie, which was destroyed by fire in February 1942. The two Queen ships were soon ordered to trooping service, for which they were refitted in Australia.

Troops of the 44th Infantry Division arrive in New York from the European battlefronts on July 20, 1945.

The Queen Elizabeth's *main lounge in the first-class accommodations.
The walls are mostly paneled with Canadian maple burr finished to a
delicate tawny pink. The large painting of Queen Elizabeth at the after
end of the lounge was placed there in recent years, replacing a marquetry
panel, which was moved to the head of the main stairs (see next
photograph). The central portion of the lounge rises 23 feet through three
decks. In the daytime the lounge is in general use by the passengers,
and occasionally there is a live or recorded concert. At night it is used
for cabaret entertainment and games, such as the traditional horserace.*

The top of the Elizabeth's *main stairs as they end at the promenade deck
square. Partly obscured by the column is the marquetry panel originally at
one end of the main lounge. Entitled "Canterbury Pilgrims," it was designed
by George Ramon and executed by an English craftsman who is listed only
as Mr. Dunn. The sculpture group above the flowers was done especially for
the* Queen Elizabeth *by Maurice Lambert. The walls of the main stairs are
paneled with Arbele, an English poplar burr. The balustrades are silver bronze.*

Typical bedroom in a first-class suite on the Queen Elizabeth.

The sitting room of a first-class suite, one of the Elizabeth's *most expensive accommodations.*

The First Class Salon or Ballroom as it appeared during the earlier years of the Elizabeth's *commercial voyages.*

The Salon was later converted into the Midships Bar, one
of the most popular cocktail lounges aboard the liner.

The First Class Restaurant,
111 feet long, 111 feet wide,
can serve more people at
one time than any other
dining room afloat. The
tapestry on the wall at
the rear was specially
designed for the ship by
two South African artists,
Eleanor Esmonde-White and
Leroux Smith Leroux.

One of the best cabin-class staterooms aboard the Elizabeth.

The cabin-class dining room, 104 feet long, 63 feet wide, accommodates 377 people at one sitting.

A typical two-berth tourist-class cabin. At first only public toilet facilities were available, but in more recent times many tourist-class cabins were renovated to include private or semi-private facilities.

The tourist-class dining saloon accommodates more than 400 passengers at a sitting.

The Observation Lounge and Cocktail Bar is one of the most beautiful rooms on the Elizabeth. *It was originally part of the first-class facilities, but later was used exclusively by tourist-class passengers.*

Another tourist-class lounge, the Winter Garden, is found on main deck.

Across the arch of heaven while you wait.
Has he answered? Does he need you at his side?
    You can start this very evening if you choose,
And take the Western Ocean in the stride
    Of seventy thousand horses and some screws!

The boat-express is waiting your command.
You will find the Mauretania *at the quay,*
Till her captain turns the lever 'neath his hand,
And the monstrous nine-decked city goes to sea.

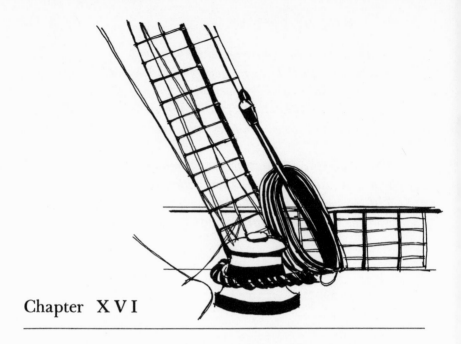

Chapter X V I

Sister Ships
in Mid-Atlantic

On Saturday, April 16, the *Queen Elizabeth* was about half-way through Voyage 424. On an 84-degree compass heading, she was cutting across the 50th parallel close to the northernmost point of the voyage. She would soon turn toward the southeast.

"Sometimes on Saturday we are able to show our passengers the *Elizabeth*'s sister ship, the *Mary*," said Commodore Marr to a visitor in his quarters that morning. "When all goes well with the weather we can sometimes come close enough to the *Mary* to see her. As you know, she is usually going in the opposite direction to the *Elizabeth.*

"But today, I am sorry to say, there is considerable distance between the two ships. I got a message this morning from her Captain, J. Treasure Jones. He left Southampton on time Thursday and is taking a course to the south of the big storm that has been causing so much trouble for shipping on the Atlantic. While we came somewhat to the north to avoid trouble, he's staying to the south for the same reason.

"Here's his message," continued the *Elizabeth*'s Master, picking up a radiogram from his desk. "The last sentence indicates that they've been feeling the effects of that storm in England. Captain Jones says here, 'Had blizzard conditions in Hampshire last Thursday.' The crocuses should be coming out there now, and here we find they're in a snowstorm."

It was too bad that the passengers on Voyage 424 missed the opportunity to see the *Queen Mary* in mid-Atlantic. Seldom in the history of the two famous *Queen* Ships has it been possible to see them at the same time, except in the middle of the ocean. The sister ships, the *Mary* and the *Elizabeth,* have been the pride of the British merchant fleet for three decades and are considered the two most famous liners to sail the seas in modern history.

The story of the beautiful *Queen* Ships began in the 1920's when Cunard, under its deputy chairman, Sir Percy Bates, decided to build two ships. Each was to be larger and faster than any passenger liner past or present. With them, Cunard would replace three older liners and, taking advantage of the new vessels' size and speed, open the first weekly passenger service across the Atlantic. The ships would be two grand, luxurious ferries plying the roughest ocean on earth.

The first was the *Mary* whose plan was started in 1926. For her designers it was a brand new experience; the *Mary* was to be a ship like no other ever constructed. She was to be so big and expensive that the existing insurance markets of Britain could not cover the vessel's full value. Therefore the Government, through a special insurance act, agreed to cover the amount that the private market dared not insure. Furthermore, the large ship would require deeper channels and larger facilities than existed at the time, so new piers were constructed in Southampton, Cherbourg, and New York. In Southampton a drydock was also built, primarily for the care of this one big ship.

Her keel was laid by the John Brown Company Limited of Scotland in December 1930, under a contract for the firm's Job No. 534 (the ship's name was a secret until her christening). A year later the Great Depression dealt a financial blow to Cunard that led to suspension of work on No. 534, and some three thousand men were unemployed in a matter of hours. At Clydebank, the construction site, the ribs of the massive new ship, gathering layers of rust, stood for more than two years as a macabre reminder of the depression. Meanwhile, the revival of Job 534 was promoted by many an Englishman as a potential means of reducing his country's unemployment and starting her on the road to recovery. Such hopes, however, were continually cut away by financial complications. David Kirkwood, the M.P. for the Clydebank area, once stood in the House and said: "I believe that as long as this ship . . . lies like a skeleton in my constituency so long will depression last in this country because as it lies there in Brown's yard, it seems to me to shout 'failure, failure' to the whole of Britain." The answer finally came when Cunard and another of Britain's big shipping lines joined to become Cunard White Star Limited, and the British Government advanced the new company a huge loan, which included money for No. 534. On April 3, 1934, the ship's construction was resumed as hundreds of workers marched into Brown's yard to the tune of a band playing "The Campbells Are Coming."

No. 534 was launched by Queen Mary on September 26, 1934, and given her name in a ceremony that for the first time saw a reigning queen name a merchant ship. As King George V and the Prince of Wales watched, the 30,000-ton hull, sliding on 200 tons of tallow and soft soap, moved stern first into the River Clyde which had been widened to accept the new giant. The event was marked by a poem set down by Poet Laureate John Masefield which, in part, read:

Long as a street and lofty as a tower,
Ready to glide in thunder from the slip
And shear the sea with majesty of power.

"It has been the nation's will that she should be completed," said King George in his speech at the launching ceremony. "And today we can send her forth no longer a number on the books, but a ship with a name in the world, alive with beauty, energy, and strength.

"Samuel Cunard [the company's founder in 1840] built his ships to carry the mails between the two English-speaking countries. This one is built to carry the people of the two lands in great number to and fro so that they may learn to understand each other. Both are faced with similar problems, and prosper, and suffer together.

"May she in her career bear many thousands of each race to visit the other as students and to return as friends.

"We send her to her element with the goodwill of all the nations as a mark of our hope for the future. She has been built in fellowship among ourselves. May her life among great waters spread friendship among the nations."

During the next two years the *Mary* was fitted out in Brown's yard. Not only did she receive machinery that would send her out as the fastest liner on the Atlantic, but she also received the expensive appointments of a super-luxurious liner. The task was left to thirty artists, sculptors, painters, and interior decorators who not only lent their artistic talents to the new liner but on occasions stirred up critical storms comparable to the worst North Atlantic weather. The *Mary* finally came down the Clyde in March 1936, went on her trials in April, and her maiden voyage in late May. She arrived in New York on June 1, 1936, to one of the greatest welcomes the city ever gave a new liner—ten years after her plans were first started.

At this time plans for the second big weekly express ship were underway. She was to be essentially like the *Queen Mary,* but with many improvements—a great deal had been learned in the decade since the *Mary* was designed. Now the French had a fabulous new liner, the *Normandie,* which won the Blue Riband (a famous prize given since 1838 to the liner with the record speed for crossing the Atlantic). The designers of the new Cunard ship felt they might learn a great deal from the *Normandie,* so they sent a spy—a naval architect— for a ride on the French liner. The man, posing as an English grocer on a holiday to America, took a thorough look at the new vessel, and at every opportunity questioned the crew about her. Thanks to this clandestine venture the *Elizabeth*'s naval architects drew considerably from the French vessel in developing what was to become the largest liner in the world.

The form of the *Queen Elizabeth*'s hull was first modeled in wax and tested in nearly eight thousand experimental sailings. These helped determine the design of the new vessel, including her propellers and rudder. The 16½-foot model was tested in a long tank at the John Brown Company, which built the *Elizabeth* as well as the *Mary.* The wax model, to simulate actual conditions, was pulled through the tank at speeds comparable to what the real ship would experience. It was even tested in simulated storms created by waves generated in the tank. Thus the *Elizabeth*'s seaworthiness was proved long before she existed. Likewise the ship's superstructure, including her stacks, were designed with the help of a wind tunnel and a detailed scale model of the ship.

Out of it all came a liner not too different from the *Queen Mary* to the layman's eye, but considerably changed from the naval architect's viewpoint. Besides many internal changes, the new plan called for elimination of the well deck, which in the *Mary*'s profile appears as an indentation of the main deck directly behind the knighthead. The change was explained in a special supplement of *The* (London) *Times* issued the day the *Elizabeth* was launched.

> One of the problems confronting the designers of the *Queen Mary* was that of dispelling the shock which might fall upon the wide forward expanse of superstructure should the *Queen Mary* decide to dip her nose in a heavy sea. The anticipated problem was solved by providing a strongly fortified well right forward into which it was calculated that such green water as came on board would fall, to lose its inertia and destructive violence by there dashing itself harmlessly into a turbulent smother of creamy foam.
>
> Throughout the most disturbed of her crossings, however, the *Queen Mary* has at no time pitched more than a relatively few degrees. She has shipped no water of any account forward, so that this forward well has proved itself a needless precaution. The *Queen Elizabeth,* therefore, will have a clean unbroken sweep of glistening deck at her forward end, a great deal more sightly to the eye than the *Queen Mary*'s well, and incidentally of greater commercial value, since it permits of the addition of some thousands of cubic feet to the useful volumetric capacity of the ship.

Eliminating the well deck was only one of several changes that gave the *Elizabeth* a longer, sleeker look than the *Mary*. New ventilating equipment for the boilers allowed the planners to leave off the sister ship's old, scooplike ventilators.

They also worked out methods for supporting the new liner's huge funnels internally rather than with a network of external guy wires. Such changes, in a sense, cleaned up the new vessel and enhanced her general look of largeness and speed.

The most obvious change in external appearance was the number of funnels. The *Elizabeth* would have two, whereas the *Mary* had three, a difference that illustrated what technological improvement had occurred in ship design in only a few years. To run its sixteen turbines geared to four propellers, the *Queen Mary* required twenty-four boilers, while the *Elizabeth*, with a similar turbine-propeller arrangement, required only twelve boilers and therefore one less funnel. The end result, of course, was more room for the payload of passengers and cargo. The *Elizabeth* was designed to carry 2,260 passengers whereas the *Mary* carried 2,038. The *Elizabeth* could also hold more cargo.

The changes added up to a ship slightly heavier and longer than the *Queen Mary*. The *Mary*'s gross tonnage measured 81,237 whereas the new ship's would measure 83,673;[1] the *Mary* was 1,019 feet 6 inches long, the *Elizabeth* would be 1,031 feet long. The 11-feet-6-inch difference would be accounted for by the *Elizabeth*'s more sharply raked prow. She would have three anchors instead of two. The center one would be held right in the prow, therefore the change in rake was to allow the anchor to fall without striking the ship's stem.

The *Queen Elizabeth* was big news in England long before her construction had begun. In fact, her first bookings were placed four months before the keel was laid and four years before the scheduled maiden voyage. At the time, in keeping with tradition, the vessel was unnamed and simply referred to by the shipyard's order No. 552. The *Queen Mary*'s name had been a well-kept secret until the moment of launching, but well before the sister ship hit the water, her

[1] A major renovation in the 1960's reduced this figure to 82,997.

name was known. Newspapers began guessing at the title even before the shipbuilding job started. In July 1936, the New York *Herald Tribune* believed the name would be *King George V*. Eventually the correct name was learned, and it was used openly. At one point someone discovered that a Thames River pleasure boat held the name *Queen Elizabeth*. To overcome this duplication, frowned upon by the British Board of Trade, the river boat was renamed *Queen Elizabeth 2*.

Workmen began laying the *Elizabeth*'s keel in December 1936. Materials flowed to her Clydebank building site from all over the British Isles. Construction plans were laid out on a weekly schedule that John Brown officials adhered to religiously, although with such a tremendous undertaking this was not easily done. Special "shock brigades" of shipbuilding specialists were organized simply to help those responsible for different parts of the ship to stay on schedule. If one section began to lag behind the others, a shock brigade was rushed there to help the regular crews catch up. Some three thousand workers used their skills in her construction, and a quarter of a million others supplied materials for the *Queen Elizabeth*. She was considered more as a national undertaking than a commercial venture.

Nearly two years from the day when workmen had begun laying her keel, the *Elizabeth,* now a 40,000-ton hull, was ready for launching. The date of the ceremony was September 27, 1938, only three days before completion of the Munich Pact and Neville Chamberlain's return to England with the declaration that the agreement had won "peace in our time." Because of Munich, the Royal Family attended the launching but the King did not. Queen Elizabeth (now the Queen Mother) came to launch the new liner, accompanied by the Princesses Elizabeth and Margaret.

While the officials and thousands of onlookers waited for the tide to peak before launching the ship, the Chairman of the John Brown Company, Lord Aberconway, was showing Queen Elizabeth the button that she should press at the proper moment to send the hull down the ways into the River Clyde. But as he demonstrated, Lord Aberconway accidentally touched the button and off went the ship.

The officials were dumfounded for a moment but then their shock suddenly changed to fear that the liner would reach the water without having been officially named. This, if tradition were followed, would leave her nameless. Lord Aberconway called to the Queen to name the ship quickly, but Queen Elizabeth replied that she had already done so. Apparently she had thought that the accidental button pushing was the way it was supposed to be, and had proceeded to do and say her part. She had released a bottle of Empire wine which had swung out on a ribbon and smashed on the liner's receding bow. As a thunderous cheer rose from the crowd, and mixed with the sounds of creaking and cracking timbers, the Queen had intoned: "I hope that good fortune may attend this great ship and all who sail in her. I am very happy to launch her and name her *Queen Elizabeth*." But her words had gone unheard for the Queen's microphone had failed to work.

As the heavy hull slid into the Clyde, she towed thousands of tons of chains behind to drag her to a stop in the river. A few of the chains, incidentally, had once served the *Great Eastern* which laid the first Atlantic cable in 1866. Once the *Elizabeth* was afloat, tugboats immediately towed the hull to a nearby fitting-out basin where she was to remain nearly two years while being finished. The date of her maiden voyage was set for April 24, 1940.

But the start of World War II, a year after the *Elizabeth*'s launching, halted her fitting-out job, and for months she stood unfinished beside the Clyde awaiting her fate. She was a prime target for German bombers: her destruction would have been considered a major propaganda victory by Hitler. And too, because she took up space badly needed for the construction of warships, it was decided that the *Elizabeth* had to be moved. The British Government released the materials and equipment necessary to complete her and in late February 1940, the job was done. Tugs hauled the second *Queen* Ship from the fitting-out basin into the Clyde which had been specially deepened to accommodate her. A few months earlier her superstructure had been painted white and her forward funnel the Cunard colors, red and black, but now the liner was completely repainted a dull, battleship gray to make her as inconspicuous as possible. While tens of thousands of people had lined the Clyde to see the *Mary* leave for the first time, hardly two dozen watched the *Elizabeth* depart her birthplace.

According to carefully laid plans, the big liner was reported to be heading for Southampton. Her special crew came from there, and had signed on with only enough personal belongings for the overnight trip to southern England. Docking plans had been made and other steps taken to receive the ship at Southampton.

But it was all a ruse. Once the liner was down the Clyde, she was anchored, and the crew was informed that the *Queen Elizabeth* was not going to Southampton but was heading to sea—the destination a secret. Most of the men agreed to go, but a few who would be caused undue hardship were allowed to return ashore.

Within the next few hours, in a quiet ceremony in the third-class dining room, the liner was turned over to Cunard, without the traditional trials that precede such a transfer. On March 2, 1940, the *Queen Elizabeth,* untried at sea, set forth across the Atlantic. She was escorted for a ways by four British destroyers and some military aircraft; then the ship set off alone in the submarine-infested ocean. Captain J. C. Townley commanded a crew of about four hundred. The ship was unarmed except for two guns on each side of the flying bridge. Though the crew did not know it, they were actually acting on an order from Winston Churchill, who had said that the liner must keep away from the British Isles until ordered to return. Indeed, the Germans, who got word of the plans, were even waiting with their bombers over the English Channel at the time the *Elizabeth* was supposed to come through on her way to Southampton.

Out at sea Captain Townley opened his secret orders to learn that he was to take the *Elizabeth* to the Port of New York where her sister ship, the *Mary,* had been caught as the war began. He was to maintain radio silence, but he would be sent important wireless communications by the Royal Navy. He was to maintain a full blackout and take an evasive, zigzag course. Regardless of his course, Captain Townley had a tremendous advantage when it came to running the Atlantic in the ship that a German U-boat crew would most love to sink. His was one of the fastest liners on earth—or at that point without trials, she was supposed to be. As he added miles between the ship and Scotland, the Master of the *Elizabeth* was rapidly convinced that she was performing as her designers and builders had planned. It would have taken an extremely clever or mighty lucky U-boat captain to sink the new *Queen.*

The *Queen Elizabeth*'s secret voyage—both her trials and her unofficial maiden voyage wrapped in one—was uneventful, yet the crew would never forget that Atlantic crossing. The vessel, sleek and new as seen from the outside, was still raw on the inside. Pipes, wires, and other materials ordinarily hidden were exposed, and some were not even fixed in place. Moreover, the gigantic ship was virtually empty, and crew members wandering around inside the liner found it a lonely, eerie experience. They made up about an eighth of the numbers the *Elizabeth* could carry when full. This new, untried grand hotel of the seas was a gray, lightless ghost ship skimming over the cold North Atlantic in the dangerous early days of World War II.

While she was en route, Cunard officials in New York were told under an oath of secrecy of the *Elizabeth*'s voyage, and that they should move the *Mauretania* from Pier 90 to make room for the new behemoth. The afternoon before her arrival, the close-mouthed officials were surprised and confused to read in the afternoon papers that the *Queen Elizabeth* was due in New York the next day. The news had come from Britain where censors had even released wireless photos of the ship as she came down the Clyde a few days before. As the wireless reports came into New York, the puzzled Cunard people were flooded with calls from newspaper reporters wanting details. But the steamship officials still felt bound by secrecy and said they had no information—which the reporters refused to believe.

That same afternoon the *Elizabeth* was sighted just east of Ambrose Light, off Fire Island, by a commercial airliner whose pilots were puzzled by this vast ship. They noted that her name had been painted over with the gray enveloping the entire hull and superstructure. The airmen were also surprised by the lack of people on such a huge vessel, for they spotted only four uniformed men on the bridge and two lonely civilians on a stern deck.

Early the next morning newspapers announced that the biggest liner in the world, the *Queen Elizabeth,* was about to enter the harbor, and thousands lined the docks to see the new ship. Above them, more thousands stood at Manhattan's office windows to see her come up the Hudson. But the *Elizabeth* missed the morning tide, so Captain Townley had to wait until 5 p.m. to enter the harbor. By then, the secret of her voyage was thoroughly compromised, and as she came up the harbor, all the ships in sight were blasting their horns in welcome, and thousands of sightseers watched and waved from Manhattan's West Side.

"Many sagas of the sea have begun and ended in our harbor," said *The New York Times;* "but can the old-timers remember anything to compare with the unheralded arrival of the biggest and fastest liner in the world after the most daring of all maiden crossings? . . . The interest of New Yorkers was echoed by the admiration of Americans everywhere for those who built her, sailed her, and sent her on her way."

In New York the *Elizabeth* met the *Queen Mary* for the first time—a meeting which was to remain one of their few encounters, other than in mid-Atlantic. At the time the two liners were expected to stay in New York for the war's duration, safe from the German bombers. But soon the *Mary* sailed for Sydney, Australia, where she was refitted for carrying troops. Next the British decided to "call up" the *Elizabeth* for trooping service, and she too sailed for Sydney and refitting.

The two ships spent the remainder of the war trooping all over the world. From November 1940 to March 1946, the *Queen Elizabeth* steamed a half million miles and carried nearly a million allied troops to and from the battle areas. At first she and her sister ship worked in the Pacific, Midde East, and Africa carrying mostly European and Australian troops. The *Mary,* in the four months of her famous "long voyage," stopped in West, South, and East Africa, Egypt, Arabia, the British East Indies, and Australia. She steamed some 40,000 miles, burned over 56,000 tons of fuel, and carried more than 30,000 troops. Another time the *Mary* carried 8,200 American troops from Boston to Sydney, while her sister ship carried 8,000 from San Francisco to the same destination. On three occasions during the war the *Mary* carried Prime Minister Winston Churchill from England to America with the Chiefs of Staff.

The *Queen* Ships eventually moved to the North Atlantic to transport American G.I.'s to the European battlegrounds. The *Elizabeth* on a wartime crossing of the Atlantic sometimes carried 15,000 or more men—an entire division. On one westbound voyage she transported 4,000 wounded soldiers accompanied by 400 doctors and nurses. On some America-bound crossings she was loaded with war prisoners. All told, the liner made thirty-four round trips on the North Atlantic, mostly between New York and the River Clyde. For years testimony to this undertaking was carried on the *Elizabeth's* teak railings where thousands of soldiers had carved their names, identification numbers, and often the names and numbers of their companies, regiments, and so on. These marks were eventually planed off the rails, and today the *Elizabeth,* with one exception, retains little evidence of her wartime service. In addition to the decorations executed by England's most famous artists of the 1930's and 1940's, on the back wall of a linen closet there is a G.I.'s drawing of a voluptuous, nude pin-up girl.

When the European war was over in 1945, the *Queen* Ships continued their trooping service, carrying tens of thousands of G.I.'s back to America. On eastbound crossings, the *Queens* often carried servicemen's families to join husbands and fathers stationed in Europe. On her last voyage connected with the war, the *Queen Mary* in 1946 carried thousands of war brides and children of American and Canadian soldiers to America.

It is not unusual today to encounter American World War II veterans whose memories of the *Queen* Ships are naturally far different from those of travelers who have experienced them as luxury liners. To the G.I. the big *Queens* were extremely crowded places. One wartime passenger was Judge Irving Levine, who now sits in the Danbury, Connecticut, Circuit Court. As a G.I., Judge Levine rode the *Elizabeth* to Scotland in the summer of 1943. On alternate nights of the Atlantic crossing he was one of eighteen fellow soldiers who shared a first-class cabin originally designed for two. On the other nights he slept on a blanket on an open deck that was so crowded that space for a reclining body was difficult to find. With everyone dining in shifts, each man ate only one full meal a day, to conserve cooks, food, and space. Judge Levine's table was located on the empty bottom of the ship's first-class swimming pool. Food was served family style, and the judge claims that men with luck such as his were always at the ends of the tables, and therefore were less well fed than those in the middle, where the full dishes of food were placed to be passed outward. Such wartime voyages cost the United States more than a million dollars each.

When the *Queen Elizabeth*'s wartime service ended, she went back to the fitting-out basin to become at last the grand Atlantic ferry she was originally intended to be. Converting the ship from war to peace duties required the removal of 260 tons of troop equipment. The wartime gray was chipped off and replaced with the traditional Cunard colors, black hull, white superstructure, and red and black funnels—all of which required 35 tons of fresh paint. One comparatively minor job in the switch from war to peace was that of cleaning blackout paint from some two thousand portholes and windows.

The *Elizabeth*'s interior accommodations had never really been completed in the eight years since her launching. When she was suddenly sent into military service, the accoutrements of a peacetime luxury liner were hurriedly disposed of. After the war, some 21,000 pieces of the *Elizabeth*'s belongings had to be shipped back to England from storage warehouses in New York and Australia.

When the finishing was done, the *Elizabeth* was finally put through the traditional tests, trials, and ceremonies that should have occurred in 1940. During the trials the ship carried Queen Elizabeth and her two daughters, Princess Margaret and Princess Elizabeth. The Royal Family was on the bridge, in fact, as Sir James Bisset, then Commodore of the Cunard Line and Captain of the *Elizabeth*, tested the liner over a measured mile. The great ship carrying the Royal Family and many dignitaries then returned from Scotland to Southampton for what is officially considered the *Queen Elizabeth*'s maiden voyage, or Voyage 1.

On this crossing, the liner was filled to capacity with 2,288 passengers, including some of the people who had booked space four years before her construction was started. Probably the most famous members of the passenger list were the Russian delegates to the newly founded United Nations, Vyacheslav Mikhailovich Molotov and Andrei Y. Vishinsky. The *Elizabeth*'s maiden voyage was a great occasion for England, so much so that it was celebrated in a poem by Sir Alan Herbert, a famous English poet, playwright, and author.

BON VOYAGE

At last, young giant, infant of the fleet
Your medals on, you sail down Civvy Street;
And may you serve the peaceful folk you bring
As well, as nobly, as you serve the King.
Here come your passengers; but who will check,
The ghosts of soldiers crowding on your deck?

The *Queen Elizabeth*'s maiden voyage was marred by tragedy. Sir Percy Bates, the Cunard Chairman who fathered the *Queen* Ships, was to sail on Voyage 1. But the morning before embarkation he collapsed in his office, and shortly before the *Elizabeth* left Southampton, Sir Percy died.

In New York, the liner received her second welcome to the harbor, but one more thoroughly planned than when the ship had surprised New Yorkers at the end of her secret

maiden voyage. In 1946 she was given the traditional welcome
with fireboats sending up dramatic sprays of water, and aircraft circling above the ship.

Following her belated maiden voyage, the *Queen Elizabeth* began her Atlantic shuttle, though she did it alone for
eighteen voyages while the *Mary* was being converted to
peacetime use. In July 1947, the sister ship was ready and the
long-delayed, weekly express service finally was underway.

The *Queen* Ships were not only the largest, most beautiful, luxurious liners on the Atlantic, but also the fastest. The
Mary held the proof. Shortly after her maiden voyage, she
took the Blue Riband away from the *Normandie* for several
months, until the French liner recaptured the prize. After a
few more months, in 1938 the *Mary* won it back and held it
until 1952. To win the prize, she covered 2,907 miles from
Bishop Rock to Ambrose in three days, 21 hours, and 48 minutes at an average speed of 30.99 knots. On the return she
made 2,938 miles between Ambrose and Bishop Rock in three
days, 20 hours, and 42 minutes, averaging 31.69 knots. Her
sister ship never outdid the *Mary* and therefore never held the
Blue Riband. It was finally lost to the new *United States* in
1952 when she crossed from Ambrose to Bishop Rock at an
average 35.59 knots.

In the late forties and fifties, the *Queen* Ships, along with
Cunard's smaller liners, carried 30 percent of the passenger
traffic on the Atlantic. Their average earnings were some
seven million a year. In the first half of the 1960's, however,
with the advent of jet planes the great steamships met with
economic difficulties. The weekly ferry service on the Atlantic, which had served well for many years, was in a poor competitive position when a jet could take a passenger to Europe
almost before a *Queen* Ship could undock and come up to
speed out at sea.

The Cunard Board of Directors in those difficult days

concluded that the basic concept for the use of Cunard liners had to change if they were to survive. In the jet age they would have to be vessels in which to entertain people as well as to transport them. Then the majestic ships might find themselves less in the diminishing business of ocean passenger service and more in the growing industry of selling ways for people to spend their leisure time.

The *Mary*, too old for a new career, was scheduled for retirement, but in the mid-1960's the *Elizabeth* was sent to Clydebank for a major renovation, to fit her out for cruising during late fall, winter, and early spring in warmer, less stormy climates such as the Caribbean or Mediterranean. During the peak summer travel season she would still work the North Atlantic carrying people between Europe and America.

Most of this major renovation had been accomplished just before Voyage 424. During a five-month visit to the John Brown yards more than four million dollars' worth of work had been done. She was newly air-conditioned. A new lido deck (outdoor sun deck) had been installed with a swimming pool on the liner's stern. And some of the *Elizabeth*'s tourist-class accommodation had undergone extensive renovations as a beginning of the effort to change her to a one- or two-class ship, instead of three, to match the more relaxed, informal attitudes of cruise passengers. Though few passengers on Voyage 424 realized it, some of this renovating work was still underway as the ship crossed the Atlantic. In a part of the tourist accommodations sealed off from the rest of the ship, a contingent of workmen were completing what they had expected to finish before the liner had to leave England.

Despite this expensive effort to keep the *Elizabeth* on the oceans, perhaps another decade, the following winter of cruising indicated she still couldn't economically justify her tonnage in the modern Cunard fleet. The grand old lady of the seas cost so much to run that she could not come home with a good profit from even the best cruise season. It was reluctantly recognized that she was more truly cast as a magnificent ferry designed for trade on the stormy North Atlantic of another age. Modern technology and social custom had changed so fast that she probably could never be renovated enough to catch up.

In the spring of 1967 Cunard announced that both *Queen* Ships would be retired, the *Mary* that fall, the *Elizabeth* the following fall.

"The impending retirement of those two elegant old ladies," said *The New York Times*, ". . . ends a glittering era in trans-Atlantic travel. The era started with the age of steam when Britain ruled the seas and continued through panics and wars, booms and depressions.

"But steam has had its day and the old ladies have become uneconomic white elephants. Just as the pomp and splendor of the railroads are no more, the age of luxurious and civilized ocean voyages is ending. The *Queens* are the last great floating hotels, obsolescent symbols for the prejet-set era."

In a couple of months the *Queen Mary* was purchased by the city of Long Beach, California, for $3,450,000, to become a maritime museum and a hotel-and-restaurant complex.

Meanwhile the sister ship was to remain in service another year while Cunard launched and fitted out a modern ocean liner. While the new vessel's hull was under construction at Brown's yard on the Clyde, she was labeled the Q4, and as the launching date approached, large bets were placed on her being christened the *Winston Churchill*. The real name remained secret until the new ship was launched by Queen Elizabeth, who christened the vessel *Queen Elizabeth 2*, much to everyone's surprise.

The new 13-deck Cunarder will be of 58,000 gross tons and 963 feet in length. Though smaller than the original *Queen* Ships, the *Queen Elizabeth 2* will have about the same passenger capacity. Because of improved ship design and engineering, she will weigh substantially less with little loss in capacity. Aluminum in her superstructure, plastic piping, lighter machinery, and new deck covering materials will help keep down her weight. The result will be a ship expected to cross the Atlantic at a service speed of 28½ knots, but will require about one half the amount of fuel as the other *Queen* Ships. The new liner's 32-foot draft will allow her to go cruising where the *Mary* and *Elizabeth* could not. She will, for example, be able to go through the Panama and Suez canals. Also her passenger accommodations will fit the modern travel market, with only one class for cruising. In the trans-Atlantic trade she will have practically one class with only a small number of "premium" passengers having exclusive use of certain public rooms. Three-quarters of her 2,025 passengers will be accommodated in outside rooms, and every cabin will have a private toilet, bath, and shower. All these improvements pretty much insure that the *Elizabeth* 2 will make profits that the *Queen* Ships were unable to bring home in their later years.

Two days after the *Queen Elizabeth* 2 went down the ways and was ready for fitting out, the *Queen Mary* left New York for the last time amid one of the largest, noisiest salutes the harbor had ever witnessed. A few months later the *Queen Elizabeth* was bought for $7,750,000 by a Philadelphia business group, who would bring her to the United States where the largest liner ever built would serve as a tourist attraction, convention center, and grand hotel.

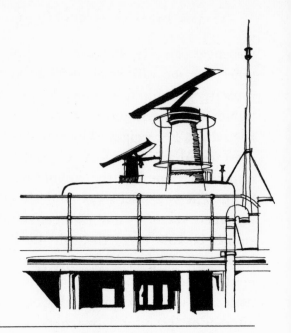

Chapter XVII

The Officers
of the Watch
Correct the Course

The first truly pleasant weather of the *Queen Elizabeth*'s Voyage 424 was encountered late Saturday afternoon, April 16, when she was steaming across a brilliant sunlit sea. The sky was filled with large cumulus clouds, and the temperature was in the fifties because of the warm North Atlantic current. A number of passengers were outside enjoying the sea air. Many, bundled in blankets, were seated in lounging chairs on the open decks, and others enjoyed some outdoor exercise by walking. One exercise enthusiast was trotting around one of the exterior decks.

For some time now the *Elizabeth*'s navigation had been conducted by dead-reckoning procedures because she was crossing the mid-Atlantic gap between the North American and European Decca radio stations. On the bridge the officers of the watch relied mainly on their gyro compass and the ship's speed for making a calculated estimate of the liner's position. They were sure of its accuracy within a few miles, but they were waiting for an opportunity to pin down the position more precisely. The chance came late Saturday afternoon as the skies cleared.

The liner's Junior Second Officer, A. C. Bennell, went onto the starboard wing carrying his own sextant, a pre-World War I model that he had purchased secondhand when he was a cadet some twenty years before. The sextant, invented in 1731, is still one of the most important navigational aids at sea. Steadying himself with his feet wide apart and with his back to the bow, Bennell "shot" the sun and returned with the data to the wheelhouse where he made his computations with the help of current nautical tables. The results allowed Bennell to locate the *Queen Elizabeth* in terms of how far east she had proceeded, but they gave him no north-south orientation. In other words, Bennell could now say that the ship stood somewhere, north or south, on an imaginary line of longitude, but he could not pinpoint her latitude. When he compared this east-west position with that figured by dead reckoning, he found the ship was estimated to be three miles ahead of her true position. Bennell then corrected the *Elizabeth*'s position on her navigational chart.

After the sun had set and the stars were out, Bennell shot the star Arcturus, the planet Jupiter, and the Pole Star. He tried for the star Regulus, but clouds obscured it. Had he been able to see only the Pole Star, he could have fixed the ship's position on a latitudinal line which he could have used with the earlier fix to pin down the liner's current position. But with his additional sightings alone Bennell figured out an exact fix, which again was compared with the dead-reckoning position. This time he found the *Queen Elizabeth*'s true location was six miles south of where she was estimated to be. Now, however, the correction required more than a change on the chart, for the liner actually had to change course twice —first to bring her north six miles, and then back onto the course she was supposed to be following. The maneuver took care of what amounted to a minor discrepancy on the vast stretches of the Atlantic.

When the course change was ordered, the *Queen Elizabeth* was being steered by an automatic pilot, which her quartermaster adjusted in order to make the turns required. For the first 72 hours of Voyage 424, the ship, because of the rough sea, had constantly been steered by one of several quartermasters, each taking his turn at the main wheel. To provide the smoothest ride possible, the man at the wheel had helped the liner ride out the wind and waves by continually applying a delicate skill earned strictly from experience, one that no machine is likely to duplicate. But now that the sea was comparatively smooth, the officers had ordered the ship onto automatic steering. This was accomplished simply by moving a lever at the side of a gray metal console housing the automatic pilot, which stands to the right of the liner's two manually operated steering wheels at the front center of the wheelhouse. The automatic device, which is gyroscopically guided, held the *Elizabeth* to the compass heading on which she stood when the machine was put to work. Then, to change course, the quartermaster only had to turn a small steering wheel on the metal console until the liner was pointed in the new direction, and there she would hold until the wheel was turned again.

While Bennell was busy placing the *Elizabeth* on her planned course, the senior man on watch, Chief Officer Victor Arbuckle, was busy with the trim of the ship. Right after he came on duty, the *Elizabeth*'s Chief Carpenter, John Bradley, arrived in the wheelhouse carryng a large chart known as the "water sounding sheet." The chart, which is filled out by Bradley and approved by Arbuckle, explained the condition of the ship's tanks. With the voyage more than half over, fuel oil and water supplies were considerably reduced, and Bradley and his crew were pumping sea-water ballast into the empty tanks to trim the ship. The sounding sheet explained his current ballast and what he proposed to do during the night. When Arbuckle had discussed the problems with Bradley and was sure he understood them, he signed the sheet, thereby accepting responsibility for what was indicated there. Bradley, who always dresses in white overalls, put the chart under his left arm, gave Arbuckle a quick salute, and left the wheelhouse. He would be back again at eight the next morning. This procedure is carried out twice daily.

A few minutes after Bradley's departure a seaman cautiously walked onto the bridge carrying a large metal tray with a big teapot, cups, saucers, and a plate of fancy cakes. He put the tray down on a counter to the starboard side of the wheelhouse, and with an abrupt salute to Arbuckle, the man left the bridge. In a moment, the two officers of the *Queen Elizabeth* were upholding the British tradition of allowing no afternoon to pass without stopping for at least a few minutes to enjoy tea. Arbuckle and Bennell, both in well-pressed blue uniforms, white shirts, black ties, and white-topped officers' caps, stood beside the tray, practically at attention, while they sipped their tea and ate their cakes. But at the same time they kept their eyes on their giant ship which was making nearly 29 knots across the bright, sunlit sea.

As two of the *Queen Elizabeth*'s eight duty officers, Arbuckle and Bennell were men working very close to the top of their profession, though the pinnacle might never be attained. Like the other duty officers, they held a master's certificate, which meant they were qualified to take over the liner's top position. Counting Commodore Marr and Captain Storey, the liner therefore had ten masters on Voyage 424, which is common for the *Elizabeth* but uncommon for many passenger steamships. All ten had been trained to become officers. None of the group had "come in through the hawsepipe," which, in nautical slang, defines the man who rises to a command position from a lowly start as a seaman before the mast. (The hawsepipe is the hole at the ship's bow which accommodates the anchor chain.)

An organization chart of the *Elizabeth*'s officers places the Commodore, of course, at the top, with the Staff Captain directly below. The Chief Officer is found immediately beneath the Staff Captain. He is above the other officers, and over the ship's carpenter, the boatswain and mates, and the deck crew, which includes the storekeeper, lamp trimmer, quartermasters, able seamen, ordinary seamen, and boys. The Chief Officer, in addition to his responsibilities for trimming the ship, is responsible for her repairs. When necessary, he sees they are done at sea; otherwise, he compiles a list of what is to be done in port.

The Senior First Officer is the Chief Officer's assistant and, through the boatswain, directs the deck crews. Next in line comes the Junior First Officer, the man in charge of all charts and other navigational aids, including the proper operation of the radar. Below him comes the ship's Senior Second Officer who acts as officer of the day (the Staff Captain's right-hand man) and is responsible for cargo and mail. Finally, the liner has a Junior Second Officer and three Third Officers who have a number of responsibilities to the Chief Officer in running the ship. One of the Third Officers acts as the ship's night officer. All eight of these officers serve two four-hour watches per day on the bridge.

At the age of sixteen Arbuckle, a native of Belfast, went to sea as a cadet for a "tramping company" (a steamship firm carrying cargo but with no fixed routes). In four years he had passed his first examinations, and he signed up with the New Zealand Shipping Company to sail on "meat boats" that took him all over the world. For instance, he frequently traveled from New Zealand or Australia to New York. Just before World War II he moved to Cunard and, with the exception of a wartime tour in British submarines, Arbuckle has been with the famous steamship line ever since. After the war he spent his life moving from one Cunard ship to another with successive promotions. By the time he became the *Elizabeth*'s Chief Officer, he had served as an officer at different levels on practically every ship of the Cunard fleet. Just prior to this latest assignment he had been twice around the world on the *Caronia*. But on the *Elizabeth*'s Voyage 424 Arbuckle was approaching another move in his professional progress. He would soon leave the liner to attend a senior officers' class on the H.M.S. *Discovery,* a yacht tied up on the Thames and used as a school by the Honorable Company of Master Mariners. With this training he expected to be given command of a Cunard cargo vessel. After a tour of duty as captain "in cargo" he expected to return to the Cunard passenger liners as a senior officer, probably as staff captain of a liner. He then could move on up to a captaincy, and should the seniority system work out that way, Arbuckle might very well become Commodore of the Cunard fleet.

CAPTAIN

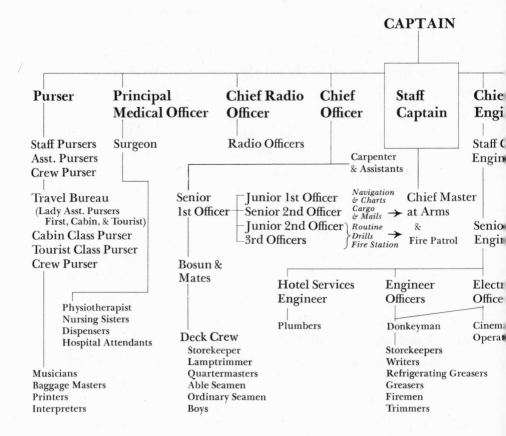

| Purser | Principal Medical Officer | Chief Radio Officer | Chief Officer | Staff Captain | Chie Engi |

Staff Pursers
Asst. Pursers
Crew Purser

Surgeon

Radio Officers

Carpenter
& Assistants

Staff C
Engin

Travel Bureau
(Lady Asst. Pursers
First, Cabin, & Tourist)
Cabin Class Purser
Tourist Class Purser
Crew Purser

Senior
1st Officer

Junior 1st Officer
Senior 2nd Officer
Junior 2nd Officer
3rd Officers

Navigation & Charts
Cargo & Mails →
Routine
Drills
Fire Station →

Chief Master
at Arms
&
Fire Patrol

Senio
Engin

Bosun &
Mates

Hotel Services
Engineer

Engineer
Officers

Electr
Office

Physiotherapist
Nursing Sisters
Dispensers
Hospital Attendants

Plumbers

Donkeyman

Cinema
Opera

Musicians
Baggage Masters
Printers
Interpreters

Deck Crew
Storekeeper
Lamptrimmer
Quartermasters
Able Seamen
Ordinary Seamen
Boys

Storekeepers
Writers
Refrigerating Greasers
Greasers
Firemen
Trimmers

THE GROUPINGS OF OFFIC

That April Saturday evening, as Arbuckle and Bennell finished their four-to-eight watch, they were anxious to join a special party that was underway in the *Elizabeth*'s wardroom. During a voyage, company rules state that officers below sen-

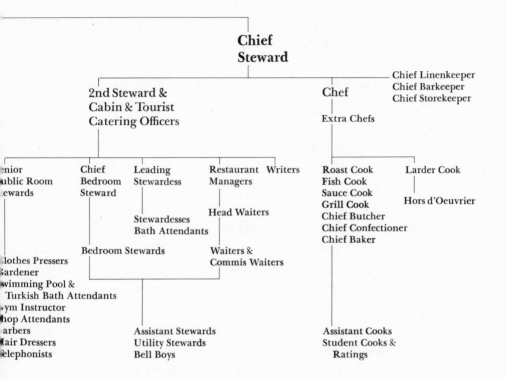

Chief Steward

2nd Steward &
Cabin & Tourist
Catering Officers

Chef

Chief Linenkeeper
Chief Barkeeper
Chief Storekeeper

Extra Chefs

enior
ublic Room
ewards

Chief
Bedroom
Steward

Leading
Stewardess

Restaurant   Writers
Managers

Roast Cook
Fish Cook
Sauce Cook
Grill Cook
Chief Butcher
Chief Confectioner
Chief Baker

Larder Cook

Stewardesses
Bath Attendants

Head Waiters

Hors d'Oeuvrier

Bedroom Stewards

Waiters &
Commis Waiters

lothes Pressers
ardener
wimming Pool &
 Turkish Bath Attendants
ym Instructor
hop Attendants
arbers
air Dressers
elephonists

Assistant Stewards
Utility Stewards
Bell Boys

Assistant Cooks
Student Cooks &
 Ratings

CREW IN A QUEEN LINER

ior levels (Captain, Staff Captain, Chief Engineer, Purser,
and so on) are not to fraternize with passengers. The one
exception is a wardroom party to which the officers are allowed to issue formal invitations. Anyone young or old, male

or female, is eligible for an invitation to the wardroom party, but prejudice rules, and invitations are limited to the most attractive young ladies aboard. From the mid-week sailing until Saturday an informal communication system gathers data which help determine the guests to whom printed invitations are delivered. The recipients are often surprised, and they seldom know how to find the wardroom, though they recognize the invitations' implications and make certain they discover the way to the party.

As they were relieved at 8 p.m., Arbuckle and Bennell hurried from the bridge to their quarters immediately below and aft. They slipped into formal dress with high, white wing collars, and then stepped into the nearby wardroom where, with four of their fellow officers, sat a model from Paris, a female French photographer and her assistant, the daughter of an English countess, an actress from New York, and several other young ladies, all of whom were most attractive. But Arbuckle and Bennell had little time to spend with their lovely guests, because it was almost time for dinner. The guests left and walked to the three different class accommodations from which they had come. The model from Paris was the only one traveling first class, so the officers accompanied her to the door of the first-class dining room. While she went to Staff Captain Storey's table, where she was an invited guest for the entire voyage, the officers proceeded to their all-male-officers' table at the forward part of the dining salon not far from where Commodore Marr sat.

A Junior Officer of the largest passenger liner in the world is strictly confined to the sailor's life, around the clock, four hours on and eight hours off, from port to port. On the Atlantic run an officer works four round trips and then receives one off, which means he is ordinarily away from home about eight weeks of every ten. If at all typical of anyone who goes to sea, he will tell you that a shore job is the only kind to have, but he won't practice what he preaches, and he'll be sailing the seas for the rest of his life.

Chapter XVIII

A Tour with the
Chief Engineer

As dawn brightened the North Atlantic on Sunday morning, April 17, the *Queen Elizabeth* stood on a course of 093 degrees, approaching the meridian of 20 degrees west, directly south of the western shores of Iceland and almost straight west of Ireland's southern tip. In a few hours her navigators would bear somewhat southeast to maintain the great circle to Bishop Rock. The sky was overcast, and occasionally the *Elizabeth* ran through a rain squall. She was still pitching slowly and easily, for the heavy swells from the great storm on the eastern Atlantic continued their march across the ocean.

It was the quietest morning of all in the liner's passenger quarters. People were sleeping because on Saturday night they had remained up later than any other night. Furthermore, time was catching up with them. At 8 a.m. ship's time, persons used to New York time were still neurologically stuck with the 4 a.m. on clocks back home.

The *Elizabeth*'s Chief Engineer, R. E. Philip, had gone to bed late but gotten up early. By 8 a.m. he had shaved, dressed, breakfasted, and was busy at work in his quarters amidships on the sun deck. Philip is a man who knows the *Queen Elizabeth*'s workings as well if not better than any man. He was even with her when she came out of the Clyde just before her secret voyage to New York in the early days of World War II. In nearly three decades since then Philip had logged hundreds of thousands of miles aboard the beautiful ship.

This morning he completed some paperwork as he awaited the arrival of a visitor, whom the Chief Engineer was to take on a tour of the liner's mechanical departments. When people are given the special privilege of looking behind the scenes, they usually want to see the engine rooms. Philip enjoys showing them around. When the man arrived, the Chief Engineer invited him to join him with a pot of coffee in his small but comfortable sitting room before going below. In the few minutes Philip talked about the passenger-liner industry.

"I don't believe that we're doomed in the age of the jet by any means. To the contrary, I feel that today's ships provide an opportunity that is very valuable. People are more and more crowded in cities. The motor car is making life more hectic. There's smog and pollution. Life is filled with pressures, and people want to get away from it all.

"On shore the chances of getting away diminish, don't

they? But out here at sea we still have a lot of space left, with clean invigorating air. So the big liners do have a place in these times, I say.

"This obviously means using our ships more for cruising, just as the company is doing. But I also believe that there can still be a good healthy passenger trade across the Atlantic. Not everybody wants to make the crossing in just a few hours by jet. There will always be passengers who like a leisurely crossing. In fact, as time goes on, the numbers who want to go by ship, to relax while traveling, could actually increase, in my opinion."

Philip tries to brief his visitors before taking them down to the engine rooms where the noise makes it difficult to hear. He picked up a piece of paper just prepared by an assistant and read off a few statistics on Voyage 424. In the first 21 hours out of New York the liner had steamed 597 miles and used 947 tons of fuel. A day later, Thursday, April 14, she had added another 652 miles and used 1,099 tons of fuel. And from Friday to Saturday she had steamed 643 miles, burning 1,039 tons. Sunday's figures, the Chief Engineer added, looked about the same.

"As we left New York," he continued, "the bridge ordered us to bring her up to 170 revolutions per minute. On the next day when we were going through all that rough weather, the bridge called for an increase to 174 revolutions to combat the weather. That, of course, ran the total fuel consumption up about 50 tons more for the day.

"To give you an idea of what it costs to speed up a ship like this let me point out that fuel consumption does not increase directly in proportion to the ship's speed, but as a cube of the speed.

"She's most efficient, we find, at about 168 to 170 revolutions a minute. Of course with weather and other problems, that isn't always possible."

The Chief Engineer next described his own department. The *Elizabeth* has twenty-two engineer officers and thirty engine ratings who work on four-hour watches in the two engine rooms and the four boiler rooms. Philip also supervises a large number of ratings who concern themselves with such matters as refrigeration, air conditioning, movies, telephones, elevators, winches, capstans, sanitary and fresh water systems, kitchen equipment, and many other technical duties.

The Chief Engineer finally reviewed the basics of what he and the visitor would see down below. The *Elizabeth,* he explained, is a quadruple-screw liner with sixteen turbines driving the four propeller shafts, each of which is some 230 feet long. There are four engines per shaft with 160,000 horsepower delivered to the four propellers. Each propeller is 18 feet 9 inches in diameter and weighs 33 tons. By themselves the propellers are a tremendous weight to whirl, but churning them around in the water three times a second truly takes immense power.

"In my department we live by engine revolutions," Philip explained. "They are carefully logged every day and totaled at the end of a voyage. As the propellers make a single revolution they theoretically push the *Queen Elizabeth* through the water 18 feet 9 inches. But then there's always resistance to overcome, and that we call 'slip.' The slip has to be subtracted from that 18 feet 9 inches.

"Let me give you the figures for a typical voyage. We count the revolutions and find the mean number for the trip, which we'll say for example is 1,162,562 revolutions. That theoretically should take the ship 3,585.3 miles, but the navigators with their charts tell us we went only 3,243 miles. The difference then must be attributed to slip, which in this case we calculate as 9.5 percent."

Philip kept rapidly piling up facts on the ship's machinery. The power transfer from each set of four turbines to a shaft is made through gears. Each gear and engine combination takes 5,000 gallons of oil to keep them lubricated properly—20,000 gallons total. All this oil is circulated, filtered, and cooled to 90 degrees for constant re-use.

Each of the twelve boilers that run the sixteen turbines has seven fires that burn a barrel of oil every twelve seconds and heat water distilled from the sea. The ship's evaporators distill twenty-five tons of ocean water an hour. Part of it goes to the liner's domestic water supply for uses other than drinking purposes. That which becomes steam for the turbines is used over and over, as many times as possible, though some is lost on each pass through the boilers. The exhaust steam from the turbines is made back into water by condensers that contain 160 miles of copper piping.

Philip, when he talks about the *Queen Elizabeth*, is encyclopedic, but time prevented his continuing. The two men put on long white coats for protection from oil and grease, which is ever present in an engine room even though crew members continually clean everything in sight. Outside Philip's quarters they took the "engineers' lift," a tiny elevator that goes down into the depths of the huge liner well below her water line. At the bottom they walked along some narrow catwalks, then down a ladder-like stairway to a metal door held tightly shut by a large steel clamp. Philip turned the clamp and opened the door which allowed him and his visitor to step into a small, dimly lit, airtight chamber on whose opposite wall was a second steel door also clamped tightly shut. Philip paused a moment to explain: "We're about to enter Number Four Boiler Room. The air inside is under pressure to assist the forced draft of our fires. The double doors prevent a loss of pressure when you come and go."

With the first door closed and fastened, Philip opened the second which suddenly made way for a blast of heat and a deafening roar. As the men stepped through the opening and closed the door behind, they were in the last of four boiler rooms, counting fore to aft. To talk to his visitor, Philip had to yell as loudly as possible close to the person's ear.

"We are running on superheated steam," shouted the Chief Engineer, "which gives you a steam temperature of 750 degrees and a pressure of 425 pounds per square inch.

"By the time it is through doing its work in the turbine, we are left with a vacuum because the steam has shrunk and dropped in temperature down around 90 to 100 degrees. We then condense it and preheat it up to around 300 degrees before returning the water to the boilers. We have to preheat it or the comparatively cold water would be too much of a shock to the boilers."

Philip led the way to where the two could look inside one of the fireboxes. They held a special dark-blue glass to look through so their eyes would not be damaged by the brilliant, white-hot fires.

"Would you believe that we even shoot steam right into that fire?" yelled the Chief Engineer. "It's something new. We now have what are called 'steam-assisted fires.' We actually inject a small quantity of steam under great pressure along with the fuel oil and oxygen. It improves the combustion and eliminates smoke. But it also uses up a lot of water that we didn't require in the past. That steam injected into the fire, of course, is then shot right up out of the funnels.

"When the boilers are steaming full, as they are right now, all the fires are going and an enormous amount of heat is made. The brickwork in the lining around the fires is red hot. In fact, it gets to the melting stage. Even if you were to put the fires out suddenly the heat in that brickwork would continue to boil the water for a long time afterward.

"This is why we can't suddenly shut down our turbines. You simply can't stop making steam very quickly. You have no way to get rid of it. Oh, you could blow the safety valves and release pressure, but this is a thing you don't do because you're then blowing distilled water into the atmosphere—and distilled water is hard to come by. So when we are coming to a stop, we take this heat off gradually. We don't lose a thing. We get the value out of it to the bitter end.

"When you're getting under way, you don't put sudden heat into this brickwork, either. You build it up gradually. Therefore, it takes time to get the ship up to speed.

"In an emergency, of course, you do anything. It depends, though, on what kind of an emergency. If someone goes overboard, you can't stop the ship anyway. But what we do is take a big circle 'round. In the meantime we can start easing things down and bring her gradually to a stop.

"But say that you had a much more serious emergency. You might make a crash stop, though it wouldn't do the machinery any good. It would mean abruptly putting superheated steam into the comparatively cold astern engines, and the sudden expansion of the turbine blades and other parts could be very damaging. But more than that it would take an enormous amount of power to reverse the propellers. While the power might be removed, remember your ship would still keep going forward. This would drag the propellers through the water and tend to keep them whirling in the same direction they were being turned by your turbines. Before you got them stopped, and going astern, all that force would have to be overcome. It would not do the gears or anything else much good.

"Emergencies, should they unfortunately occur, would of course take a lot of fast and good thinking here in the engine department."

From Number Four Boiler Room, the Chief Engineer led the way forward through Number Three Boiler Room and into one of the ship's two electric power plants which separate Boiler Rooms Two and Three. Eight turbine-driven generators are tightly fitted into the two areas. Their total capacity is nearly 9,000 kilowatts, enough to meet the electric needs for a small city. In the *Elizabeth* the electricity flows to 30,000 light bulbs through more than 4,000 miles of wiring. In addition to the lighting demands, the ship contains about 650 electric motors, that range from a fraction of a horsepower up to 360 horsepower.

Next the two men came to a port stabilizer installation. It is one of four that operate two fins on each side of the hull. The interior equipment for each fin is contained in a small compartment, tightly packed with machinery, but it is a quiet place compared to the boiler and generator rooms. The stabilizers were installed in 1955 with much difficulty. Four spaces, two on each side of the ship, had to be found within the already crowded hull. Around these areas the ship's structure had to be strengthened tremendously to hold the 20-ton components and endure the forces which would be placed upon the moving hull when a fin is held out into the sea. The installation work at the ship's Southampton drydock presented interesting problems. The equipment was too large to lower down through the ship so it had to be inserted through large holes cut in the steel hull. But even this was an uncertain approach because space between the hull and drydock was barely enough to accommodate the new machinery. To make certain that it could be done, the engineers first proved their plan on scale models of parts of the *Elizabeth* and the drydock.

"In this stabilizer unit," the Chief Engineer explained, "we have four hydraulic rams that have enough power to extend the fin through the side of the ship into the water. And that takes some power, considering you're forcing an object of considerable size out into the water while the ship is moving at top speed. The fin sticking out of the hull, controlled by this equipment, reaches twelve and a half feet out into the water, and it is just over seven feet wide. It takes about two minutes to get the fins out after the order comes down from the bridge. They can be retracted in a minute and a half.

"When we're moving along at full speed and the fin tilts—it's done electrically—a force of up to 110 tons can be exerted on the sides of the ship. You can understand why this area of the hull around the installation needed strengthening.

"We're standing between the two after fins which are more powerful than the forward set. At this point the ship is wider than where the forward fins are located, so these have more purchase on the vessel when they're actuated."

As Philip explained the stabilizers, they were still in operation, and the machinery countered the ship's attempts to roll. Large, electrically actuated arms moved up and down as the outside fin was revolved a few degrees one way, then the other, to maintain the ship as level as possible. The arms moved irregularly, as though they were sensing the varying forces of the ocean in order to accomplish their purpose.

"The four fins are coordinated electrically," added Philip. "Each of the four fins has an 80-horsepower electric motor to actuate it. The motors are coordinated through an electrical system that works in conjunction with the gyroscopes at the heart of the stabilizers.

"The drag of the extended fins, of course, affects the speed of the ship—slows her down about a half knot. But what is lost in speed is likely to be gained in distance. The ship, riding more smoothly, can stay on course much better, and thereby she is enabled to take the shortest route to where she is going."

Philip led the way back through the two after boiler rooms to the forward engine room where again the Chief Engineer had to shout: "On each side of the ship here you have a unit of four turbines, all four of which are geared to one of the ship's four propeller shafts. The turbines that are running right now are the ones driving her forward. The units also include the turbines to drive her astern, but they're receiving no steam.

"We have eight turbines in this section of the ship, and as we walk aft, we'll pass two additional units with eight more turbines. Together the sixteen turbines give us the ship's 160,000 horsepower on her four shafts."

In each of the engine rooms Philip greeted the crewmen in charge. They worked at large control panels beside the operational ends of the ship's telegraphs controlled from the bridge. The telegraphs were set at "Full Ahead," and the in-exorable roar of the powerful turbines told the full story of this engine setting when applied to the world's largest liner. Incredibly powerful forces were at work pushing the *Elizabeth* at 28½ knots over the mid-Atlantic on what elsewhere was a quiet Sunday morning.

Philip's tour continued back through the two engine rooms, and out onto a catwalk between the propeller shafts. The silently whirling cylinders of steel, 27⅝ inches diameter, polished like mirrors, appeared to turn with great ease considering the fury of fire and steam on the turbine end and the violently churning water at the propeller end.

"You can imagine the force the propellers have to exert upon the water to push a ship like this," said the Chief Engineer. "That means a counterforce is pushing directly back from the propellers through these shafts, and it has to be absorbed by the ship from the shafts. It can't be absorbed by the gears at the end of a shaft because they couldn't take it. It is done through metal collars—raised metal ridges encircling the shaft—that ride enclosed in circular metal channels attached to the ship's structure. These channels, called 'pads,' hold the shaft from moving backwards or forwards, except for a very little bit—only one sixty-thousandth of an inch—and they absorb the force from the propellers and transmit it to the ship.

"But that sixty-thousandth play is important as the ship pitches and hogs and sags—bends in the middle, you know. That small opportunity for the shafts to play back and forth prevents a shaft from having to bend with the ship—which could be a serious matter in terms of the vibration it would produce."

Proceeding along the catwalk, Philip pointed to a device that straddled one of the revolving propeller shafts. He explained that it was an electrical-mechanical sensing device that registers how much horsepower is being developed on each shaft. It measures how much the metal of the shaft is being twisted by the forces revolving it. Of course, the twist is very minor, but the equipment is extremely sensitive. The amount of twist is translated into horsepower on dials in an engine room up forward.

Soon a bulkhead prevented the men from walking further aft. Philip said that the rudder end of the *Elizabeth*'s steering system was beyond the bulkhead and to enter the compartment was inadvisable, except in an emergency. The space houses a heavy tiller actuated by a powerful electro-hydraulic system. And certainly it has to be powerful, for the liner's great rudder weighs 140 tons, which, as is often pointed out, is heavier than the Pilgrims' ship, the *Mayflower*. The tiller is swung by four hydraulic cylinders designed to continue working in twos should the two others ever fail. If all the cylinders fail, provision is made for a direct mechanical link between the manual steering wheels on the bridge and the tiller. But in normal operation, the system requires that the helmsman strain no more than a little finger to turn his wheel and bring the 83,000-ton liner around.

At this point the Chief Engineer spent a couple of minutes talking about the differences in helmsmen, especially in a rough sea. The older, more experienced quartermaster is usually relaxed at the wheel and turns it as little as possible.

The younger, less experienced man is likely to keep the wheel going all the time and the job is much more taxing.

"Let me assure you," said Philip, "that the young man is absolutely competent or he wouldn't be there. But it does take years before you learn to handle this ship in a rough sea like the older man. He has come to know the sea a lot better; he doesn't fight it.

"The average passenger I doubt would ever notice this in the feel of the ship, but I can. When the older, more experienced hand on the wheel is replaced by the younger, less experienced one, I can tell practically the second it happens. I can tell by a change in how the ship feels and sounds. When the rudder is turned too much, it of course is dragged through the sea against the ship's forward motion. That, for a moment, produces a vibration reflected through the ship. I notice it, perhaps on a subconscious level, but I do. If the vibration lasts too long, I would certainly give it serious thought, but it is only momentary.

"This less experienced helmsman is somewhat rougher on the ship's machinery than the older man, too. As the young helmsman forces the ship to fight the sea rather than going with it, he likewise calls for surges of power, which is always harder on machinery. The more experienced helmsman, holding her steady, doesn't put the same demands on the machinery. Now you see why the engine department learns how the ship is being handled from the sound and feel of things."

Back in Philip's quarters up on sun deck he poured some drinks before lunch, and then picked up his earlier talk about the future of ocean liners.

"Mechanically a ship like the *Mary,* or *Elizabeth,* could undoubtedly be kept going indefinitely, if you wanted to pay the price. But what brings them down are the economic factors of technological change. Today's modern ships can be just as powerful and just as fast with modern turbines that are much, much smaller than what you have just seen. They'll drive the ship as well, but leave a lot more space for payload, or improved crew quarters. Also, automation is coming into modern ships. My engine department today requires a large staff, but a lot of the work certainly can be automated.

"Computers may play a part, but I doubt if you can ever completely eliminate the human factor in a ship. A trained person can smell, he can hear. These are things down there in the working parts of the ship that matter greatly. You can smell an oily bearing before it flies up and you lose it. You can hear and act on a change of note. A set of gears has a certain sound while another set—supposedly a duplicate set—has another sound. A trained person learns to recognize these minor differences, and if they change in note he knows what to do. No computer, at least from what I know, is likely to be doing this sort of thing on a ship."

But anyone with the rare opportunity to take the Chief Engineer's tour during a voyage does not come away thinking about computers. The impression is one of massive, deafening machinery maintained by men with strong, grease-stained hands wielding man-sized wrenches, hydraulic jacks, and hammers. One leaves with the feeling that the *Elizabeth*'s serviceability comes from a tremendous investment in strength from massive iron and steel parts. With the strong men maintaining the strong parts she has run and run, mile after mile, night and day, through nearly three decades of the roughest ocean on earth.

The ship, however, has rested from her travels about a month a year, but even then she has been given little peace. In the winter the *Elizabeth* is usually drydocked in Southampton for her annual overhaul. Her underwater sides are scaled and completely inspected. The propellers are removed so that the shafts can be looked at, and everything else that can't really be inspected during operation is given a thorough going-over.

The ship swarms with workmen, often around the clock. At this time she may be changed in some substantial way. One year her tanks were altered to allow her to carry more fuel oil. The fins were added during a drydocking. Finally, some eight tons of paint are applied to the great ship, and she goes back to sea.

A few minutes after twelve o'clock a man delivered a printed form to the Chief Engineer who quickly surveyed it.

"At noon," Philip explained, "a 'run chit' is always sent to me from the bridge. Everything about the ship's mechanical operation is written on the chit: propeller revolutions for the day, the miles we've traveled according to propeller revolutions, the average revolutions per minute, fuel-oil consumption, and oil remaining in the ship.

"These records for Voyage 424 show that our roughest days on fuel consumption were in the beginning. On the first day out, during the roughest part of the trip when we were steaming into a heavy sea, the propeller slip was 13.3 percent. In the next couple of days it dropped to around 11.8. This reveals how the ship had a fight on her hands in the beginning. Today that percentage I expect will even be down between nine and ten percent."

While the Chief Engineer was below, an order had come from the bridge to reduce propeller revolutions from 170 to 164. The Commodore had decided that he now had more than enough time to make Cherbourg on schedule the next day. By reducing revolutions he could still arrive on schedule, yet save fuel.

At this midday hour, the *Queen Elizabeth*'s navigators were taking her slightly to the southeast. She was approaching the meridian of 15 degrees of west longitude, southwest of Fastnet, on the southern tip of Ireland.

Chapter XIX

A Sunday with
the Commodore

Religious services were conducted all morning on the British liner that Sunday, April 17. In the *Queen Elizabeth*'s lounge, Anglican and Episcopalian rites were held at 8 o'clock. No Roman Catholic priest was aboard, so the Catholic service had to be limited to saying the rosary at 9:30. The largest attendance of all was at the nondenominational services held in the main lounge at 11 o'clock. With the weather now quite favorable, Commodore Marr came down from the bridge to conduct the service. It is a shortened version of the

Church of England morning service and is always conducted by the liner's captain, or another senior officer if the top man is unable to attend. To avoid any clerical conflicts, especially when more than one clergyman is on the ship, Cunard has maintained the "polite fiction" that this is the company's service for the ship's captain to conduct. And the fiction has been rigidly held to, even when the *Queen* Ships have carried the Archbishop of Canterbury. For Voyage 424, Commodore Marr's service included a special prayer from the Church of Scotland to be used while at sea. Whenever the Queen of England was mentioned in the prayers, the Commodore added: "And the President of the United States." The ship's Master also selected hymns from a special selection written for worshippers at sea. He obviously enjoyed his clerical role.

From the service the Commodore returned to the bridge and then back to his quarters where he was served lunch. Later that afternoon he was visited by an old friend, a passenger long experienced with ocean-liner travel. He had been invited to come by the Commodore's quarters for tea. They sat for some time talking, mostly about the past, and the *Elizabeth*'s Master recounted some of the stories about his life that he best likes to tell.

Little in the early family history of Geoffrey Thrippleton Marr would indicate that he would become the top sea captain of the British Merchant Marine. "I was born in Pontefratt in Yorkshire, sixty-eight miles from the sea," says the Commodore. "My family was, you might say, non-seafaring. My mother's people were all shopkeepers; my father's were farmers.

"I doubt that they ever thought of me as a seafaring type, either. I was a sickly child. I was not regarded as being very strong. I had a weak chest. I wasn't allowed to go to school until I was seven years of age.

"But I used to be sent every summer to my maternal

grandparents who had a summer home in the little fishing village called Robin Hood Bay, on the northeast coast. I think it was during these long ago days that I spent at Robin Hood Bay—talking to the fishermen there and going out in their boats and talking to the retired sea captains—which created an interest in the sea that has never left me. I soon had no other idea but to go to sea."

At the age of fourteen, in September 1922, Geoffrey Marr became a cadet on the training ship H.M.S. *Conway,* where he spent two years. For the next twelve years, young Marr worked for an English subsidiary of the United Fruit Company. During this time he passed examinations for all the certificates required to become a ship's master. From there he transferred to the Cunard Steam-Ship Company in 1936 as Junior Third Officer of the *Andonia.*

At the outbreak of World War II the future Commodore was an officer on the new *Queen Mary* which was en route to New York. Upon arrival, the liner was tied up, supposedly for the duration of the war, and her officers waited for orders. For the first five months of the war, Marr lived in New York aboard the luxury liner, and then was ordered home to join the Royal Navy.

He had a varied and exciting naval career during World War II, for which he received the Distinguished Service Cross in 1946. When the Commodore talks about his wartime service—as he is likely to do with each new group of guests at the Captain's table—two major events usually come to his mind: Dunkirk, and the sinking of the *Bismarck.*

On the third day of Dunkirk, Marr, having recently returned from the *Mary,* went to Ramsgate where the famous evacuation fleet was being mounted. He was put in command of a refueling mission with a drifter, a small fishing vessel, carrying 400 cans of gasoline. His orders were to avoid Dunkirk's heavily bombarded main channel and to come into the beach over sandbars to the north at high tide. Once there, Marr found some crucial buoys missing, but decided to proceed without their aid. After temporarily getting stuck on a sandbar exposed to German bombers and artillery, he headed around to the main channel, which seemed to be the only possible route to the Dunkirk beach. However, on arrival he found comparatively few crews willing to stop to refuel during the bombing, so the Cunard officer, still with half his gasoline, picked up two hundred soldiers and took in tow four disabled vessels, all heavily loaded with evacuees.

"We put off, rather like a string of chickens," recalled Commodore Marr. "This was about one o'clock in the morning. I was navigating by the light of fires from oil storage depots at Dunkirk which the German bombers had hit. A number of ships had been sunk, and I was navigating around the wrecks of Dunkirk. It was an eerie sight.

"Finally we got to the channel and set off, stemming the tide at about four knots. The channel was about twelve miles long. As we went out, a flotilla of destroyers came in. They were shelling the German guns behind the town. But the German guns opened up at the destroyers, and we were caught in the middle. With all those boats in tow, we were in a very tough spot with shells falling all around. But somehow we got through, and we made it back to Ramsgate the next afternoon.

"That was the last time any small vessels were able to get into Dunkirk. It was one of the turning points in British history I was able to take a part in."

A year after Dunkirk, Commodore Marr was involved in the sinking of the *Bismarck* by H.M.S. *King George V*, the British battleship to which he was assigned. "It was a critical period for Britain," says the Commodore. "Had the battle with the *Bismarck* gone the other way, it could have been a turning point in the war, because the blow to British morale would have been so great.

"Not only was I fortunate in being present at this action, but in being one of the few officers able to watch the whole of the battle without having anything else to do. I was assistant navigating officer on the *King George V*. It so happens that in this class of ship, when the men are on action stations, the assistant navigator's duties include manning a secondary conning position, which was a little secondary bridge. Had the main bridge been put out of action, I would have been able to take over temporary command of the ship. As the bridge was not hit, I had nothing to do, except watch the battle.

"We opened fire at a range of approximately 30,000 yards, about fifteen sea miles. We closed the range steadily until ordered to cease fire at a range of about five miles, which is point-blank for the guns of such battleships.

"Through my binoculars I was able to see that the *Bismarck* was on fire, fore and aft. It was a holocaust of flame. She was only firing sporadically. I could actually watch her crew running along the deck and jumping into the sea.

"The order to cease fire was given and the *King George V* and the *Rodney*, the two British battleships in the action, turned away and the signal was made to the cruiser *Dorsetshire* to close on what was literally just a hulk and sink her with torpedoes.

"Through my binoculars I watched the *Bismarck* finally roll over and sink as we steamed away, which was a sad end to a very gallant adversary who had come out against great odds determined to sell her life dearly.

"I still believe the *Bismarck* was the finest fighting machine the world has ever seen, or ever will see in battleships. Not only was this a historic turning point in history, but it was the last of the classic naval engagements with gunnery duels between battleships."

On the *Queen Elizabeth* Commodore Marr carries a chart of the Atlantic marked with the routes and the various points of action that occurred in the chase and sinking of the *Bismarck*. Often at his table, or at special gatherings in his quarters, he tells the complete account of the action, using the chart to clarify the story.

"That was the highlight of my war service career," says Commodore Marr, "which included Russian and Gibraltar convoys, and other widespread duty tours. It was a great honor to be present."

From the Navy, he returned to the Cunard liner *Mauretania* as an officer and a few months later was put in his first company command position, as master of a cargo ship. From there until he reached the top, his career followed the traditional pattern up through the ranks. A few years of commanding cargo vessels, and he became a staff captain, serving on the *Queen Mary*, the *Queen Elizabeth*, and the *Caronia*. His first permanent command of a passenger liner was on the R.M.S. *Scythia*, and then he commanded the *Ivernia*, the *Parthia*, the *Carinthia*, and the *Caronia*, the last of which he took around the world. Next he became "relieving captain" for the two *Queens*, then Captain of the *Queen Mary* in 1965, followed by his being named Commodore of the Cunard Line and Captain of the *Elizabeth* just prior to the liner's Voyage 424.

The Master of the *Queen Elizabeth* speaks humbly of his title as Commodore of England's prize merchant fleet. "It is only a courtesy title," he says, "given to the senior captain of the line—as is true in most shipping companies. It doesn't mean much more than managing to join the company at the right time and staying out of trouble long enough to become

the senior captain. It is the title conferred by the manage-
ment, and it carries a small increase in pay."

While the passengers see the captain of a great liner like
the *Elizabeth* or *Mary* at dinner and social functions, the true
tests of the job, of course, are usually on the bridge. He cannot
forget that his is the final responsibility for the ship. While
maritime laws and company rules set limits to guide the ship's
captain, in the end his judgment is supreme.

One day in 1965, as master of the *Queen Mary,* Captain
Marr was faced with hours of painful decision-making that so
often go with such a command. On a westbound voyage to
New York, the *Mary*'s radio brought word that a nearby
Greek freighter, the *Constantis,* was in trouble. Her captain
wanted to abandon ship, fearing that she was about to break
up in the extremely rough seas and rugged westerly gale
winds. She was some 450 miles off Bishop Rock. Captain Marr
decided to go to the ship, though he knew the rough seas
would undoubtedly prevent his helping the crew in any way.

When the *Mary* came in view of the *Constantis,* the latter
was trying to hold into the wind, but the gale was actually
blowing her back toward Europe at four or five knots. Upon
seeing the huge *Queen* Ship, the freighter captain immediately wanted to take his crew by lifeboats to the liner. However, Captain Marr, feeling this would be foolhardy, radioed
the Greek shipmaster to stay with the ship at least until it was
absolutely certain she would break up.

The cargo captain accepted the advice, but insisted on
the *Queen Mary* staying by him, and Captain Marr agreed.
All through the night the big Cunarder remained in sight of
the *Constantis.* But as the night progressed, the *Mary*'s Captain began to get extremely worried. Instead of proceeding to
New York, he was actually being blown back toward his point
of departure, while continuing to burn fuel. Moreover, the
weather reports indicated the *Mary* would have to fight strong

westerly winds all the way to New York, which would increase fuel consumption. As morning came, the *Mary*'s Captain, responsible for thousands of passengers and crew, knew he had to depart.

The sight of the beautiful liner, her lights blazing all night across the stormy sea, had given the *Constantis* Captain the courage he needed so that by morning, when he was told the *Mary* was leaving, he felt better about sticking with his ship—which remained intact. He radioed a message of gratitude and good-bye to the *Mary*'s Master as the liner steamed away to the west.

The voyage from there to New York, however, was a nerve-racking business. The percentage of slip with his propellers fighting the storm was extremely high—and so therefore was fuel consumption. Calculations showed that at best the *Mary* would come into New York with barely enough oil to steam up the harbor. To conserve his supply, Captain Marr ordered the engine revolutions reduced drastically, which saved fuel, but prolonged the agony of wondering whether the ship could make it or not.

As the *Mary* picked up the Sandy Hook pilot at Ambrose, she had but 356 tons of oil left in her bunkers, and the Chief Engineer was reminding Captain Marr that at 150 tons the supply could not be pumped. So when the *Mary* came up the Hudson that day, many hours late, she was truly close to being without power.

On such a voyage, or any trip at sea with a large ocean liner, the master must have the kind of nerves that allow him to sleep, or by the end of each voyage he might come apart like unraveling strands of a braided wire. The secret, says Commodore Marr, is the ability to trust one's officers. "If you don't learn such trust," he explains, "you're going to wear yourself into a fit of exhaustion. I do trust them, and I sleep very well.

"But that doesn't mean you always come home refreshed. I feel a voyage tends to build up a certain amount of nervous tension, especially toward the end. Last time we came home we ran into fog and low visibility in the English Channel, while they were having nice clear weather in England. I was up most of the night. Then we had to go into Cherbourg in the morning. I got home that evening feeling very tired. That of course came from no sleep the night before, then a very full day when you've got to get all your reports out. But after a little sleep at home, I get out in the garden which I find most relaxing."

In recompense, the Commodore says, life at sea is always exciting, always offering something new, each crisis a different one. "It is very much a man's job," he concludes.

Through it all Commodore Marr has found that the spirit of what he does is best said in poetry. His two favorite poets are John Masefield and Rudyard Kipling. Masefield went to the same training school as Commodore Marr, intending to be a seafarer. Kipling's poetry, in the Commodore's mind, especially catches the flavor of the sea. That Sunday afternoon on Voyage 424, while talking to his friend, he recited the first verse from one of his favorite Kipling poems, "White Horses," which describes the white tops of waves.

> *"Where run your colts at pasture?*
> *Where hide your mares to breed?*
> *'Mid bergs about the ice-cap*
> *Or wove Sargasso weed;*
> *By chartless reef and channel,*
> *Or crafty coastwise bar,*
> *But most the ocean-meadow*
> *All purple to the stars!"*

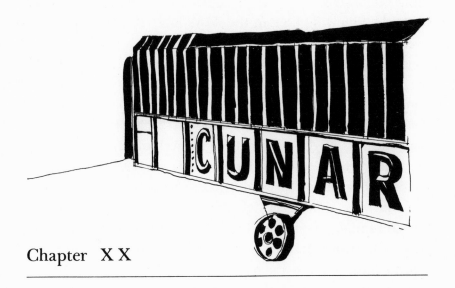

Chapter X X

Cherbourg

Sunday afternoon and evening the *Queen Elizabeth* steamed more and more southeast until a few minutes before midnight when her navigators made their last course alteration before Bishop Rock by bringing her to a heading of 106 degrees. Navigational fixes were now obtained with the Decca Navigator tuned to the European network of Decca stations, and this system revealed that the *Elizabeth* was directly south of Ireland. The fury of the storm that had smashed the *Michelangelo* was gone, though it had been here a few days earlier, as the sea indicated. On the eight-to-twelve watch the duty officer made the following note in the ship's log: "Rough sea. Heavy swells. Showers."

As the *Elizabeth*'s clocks were advanced at midnight for the fifth time during the voyage and it suddenly became one hour into April 18, a growing sense of anticipation was evident on the darkened bridge. The watch officers went about their business in the wind-battered wheelhouse, moving from the lighted charts to the radar enclosure, to the Decca set, but continually glancing forward into the darkness.

Since the Nantucket lightship, sighted the first night out, the ship's night watches had not seen another light on the sea across the entire Atlantic. They had spotted several ships or fishing boats on the radar, but they had never been close enough, nor had the atmosphere been clear enough, for lights to be visible. But now the men knew that Bishop Rock was not far away. When the inbound English sailor sees Bishop Rock, though he still has miles to go, he is home, for he is looking at the southwest extremity of his motherland. Outbound he is saying a final good-bye. Near Bishop Rock large liners often begin to slow down on the way into Europe, or let out their speed when leaving.

In about an hour the darkness that had prevailed for so many nights was finally broken by a distant, dim light off the starboard bow, barely a speck in the blackness of night. The radar screen indicated it was a ship, undoubtedly a freighter, proceeding from the English Channel into the Atlantic. She never did come close, nor did her lights grow any brighter as they appeared to move around the *Elizabeth*'s starboard beam, until they disappeared off her starboard quarter. But that was only the beginning of the lights. From then on, one, two, or three were continually visible around the *Elizabeth* as she plowed on toward the point in the sea just south of Bishop

Rock over which so many ships pass en route to and from
Europe.

As the watch changed at 4 a.m., and the liner's Chief
Officer, Victor Arbuckle, took over, all the men and officers
kept looking off the port bow for the flashing light on Bishop
Rock. It was first seen at exactly 4:10 and entered in the ship's
log. In a few minutes, Arbuckle ordered the helmsman to
alter course from 106 degrees to 089, which brought the *Elizabeth* around the Scilly Isles and pointed her bow up into the
English Channel.

"Another fabulously successful job of navigating the
North Atlantic," said Senior Third Officer Dootson with a
laugh. He had delayed leaving the wheelhouse from his
midnight-to-four watch in order to see the first sighting of
land on Voyage 424.

"Good job, fellow," said Arbuckle. "You can go back to
bed."

Shortly after passing Bishop Rock the *Elizabeth*'s officers
began watching a vessel coming up on her port bow, obviously
a large ocean liner. As she moved closer to the big Cunarder,
her multiplicity of lights became evident.

"It could be the *United States*," said Bennell.

"Not this week," said Arbuckle. "She was heading into
New York when we were going out on the Bermuda cruise. I
say she is the *France*."

As the westbound liner, many of her portholes and windows brightly lit, approached through the night, it was clear
the two ships would pass near one another. In a few minutes
the unknown vessel was off the *Elizabeth*'s port bow, and suddenly she gave a dramatic greeting. Her officers flashed the
ship's display lights on and off twice. The brilliant spotlights,
used to display the liner's stacks and superstructure at night in
port, illuminated the sea, and for those two moments, the pass-

ing vessel in all her colors, and all her beautiful lines, was impressed on the black screen of night.

"The *Bremen!*" said several voices at once in the *Elizabeth*'s wheelhouse, and in return the British ship's display lights were flashed twice. Then the dark outlines of the huge liners glided quickly by one another, two fast-moving hotels of the sea, with the reflections of their hundreds of lights prancing along the waters roiled by their passage. The German liner was heading out to New York after a stop that afternoon at Cherbourg.

An hour later the protracted job of slowing the *Queen Elizabeth* down began when an order from the bridge asked the engine department for a reduction in propeller revolutions to 138 from the 164 they had been turning since the previous day. Thus during the morning, beginning around 5 a.m., the liner's turbines were slowed down a little at a time until they were back to the 100-per-minute maximum for maneuvering revs.

As the *Queen Elizabeth* enroute to Cherbourg steamed slowly through the Channel waters south of Cornwall, Devon, and Dorset, the sun rose in a clear sky. It was to be a beautiful day for the landing in Europe. The liner's passengers had missed such weather for five days, and they wanted to get outside, but those disembarking in France were busy with final packing in their cabins. At 9 a.m. bedroom stewards began carrying the bags to central points from which they could be rapidly removed out over the gangways at Cherbourg.

Commodore Marr ate breakfast as usual in his quarters and, after doing some chores at his desk, he went to the bridge. The liner was coming into view of the French coast. The wheelhouse doors were open and the officers went out onto the starboard wing where, for the first time since New York, the weather was truly enjoyable. First in sight was a lighthouse on a tiny speck of land, Casquets, west of the island of Alderney, in turn west of the Cotentin Peninsula and the port of Cherbourg. On this extremely pleasant morning the distant land was a brilliant green. Once more the *Elizabeth* was soon gliding silently through the water in her approach to a docking, but what a difference here compared to steaming up New York Harbor and the Hudson. In place of the towering concrete-and-glass buildings, the unfolding view was one of beautiful, rich farmlands bathed in the morning sunlight.

"We are back in the butter-and-egg country," said Commodore Marr to one of his officers as they looked over the rural scenery spreading gently up from the Normandy coast, well known for dairy products.

In a little while the Commodore ordered his crew onto docking stations. Officers, quartermasters, engineers, and messengers went to the various points they would man during the landing in Cherbourg. Once more the bridge had an air of formal solemnity which had not been noticeable since these same men were at the same stations, back in New York. Everyone stood quite stiffly at attention. Talking was limited, and then it was held to whispers. And again the Commodore, wearing his long bridge coat, walked about, occasionally holding a brief conversation here or having a word with an officer there. Below the bridge the forward main deck was busy with deck hands unbattening hatches and preparing the mooring lines for the docking. In the rigging on the forward mast, directly in line with the bridge, men were working to unlash the lines that would be used to discharge cargo at Cherbourg. At the helm, as he had been in New York, was Chief Quartermaster Charles Ernest Bell. In his round white-topped Cunard hat he looked very much the old English salt. And he had every right to the part, for he had begun going to sea in the 1920's. Until World War II he was a North Atlantic fisherman and a crewman on cargo vessels. During the war he commanded mine sweepers out of Dover, one of which he brought into Normandy along the treacherous Juno Beach east of Cherbourg during the 1944 Allied invasion.

About three and a half miles from where the ship enters the French port, the city, dominated by Fort du Roule on a nearby bluff, came into view. In its rural setting it looked more like a country village than a major European seaport. Between the distant city and the *Queen Elizabeth* a small launch was bobbing over the waves coming toward the oncoming liner. The boat carried the Cherbourg pilot who would take the *Elizabeth* from the open sea through an outer and inner breakwater and then dock her at a large, modern quay for trans-Atlantic liners.

"Dead slow ahead!" commanded the Commodore as the pilot boat moved in on the liner. The *Queen* slowed down to practically a stop to take on the pilot, Captain Jean Burel, who, in a few minutes, entered the wheelhouse where he shook hands with Commodore Marr and greeted the officers and crew. Captain Burel, who speaks English with a heavy French accent, is the one of Cherbourg's five licensed pilots who usually handles the British *Queen* Ships. The five pilots form an association, called the Syndicat des Pilotes, which, on a small scale, is comparable to the Sandy Hook Pilots Association. The Syndicat des Pilotes owns two pilot boats, a rugged one for winter and a lighter one for summer use. The winter boat had just put Captain Burel aboard.

"We have a nice stiff wind, Pilot," said Commodore Marr. "It's about twenty knots, gusting thirty to thirty-five. Do you feel we will have any difficulties?"

"I do not think so," said Captain Burel. "We should get no trouble today, I think."

At Cherbourg, Commodore Marr is usually concerned more about wind than tides. At neap tide a *Queen* Ship can enter or leave the harbor at any hour, and at spring tide she is free to come or go except within two hours of low water. Furthermore, the force of the tides at Cherbourg have little influence on a ship once she is beyond the breakwaters in the well-protected inner harbor, the Petite Rade. However, the harbor is not very well protected from the westerly winds that cut across the Cotentin Peninsula at a right angle to the quay for trans-Atlantic liners. This can give a *Queen* Ship trouble as the wind sweeps around the large terminal building, the Gare Maritime, on the quay. When the liner approaches, her bow moves into the lee of the building, but her stern, some 1,100 feet aft, remains in the full force of the wind. If the pressure on the stern is great enough, it can whirl the liner, swinging the after end away from the quay. Therefore, with strong westerly winds, docking at Cherbourg is considered inadvisable, especially because the port's tugboats are not strong enough to cope with the huge liner under these tricky circumstances. In high winds the *Queen* Ships are anchored in the harbor away from the quay, and passengers disembark on one of five tenders. But in the year previous to the *Elizabeth*'s Voyage 424, she had had to discharge passengers by tender only twice.

The winds of Cherbourg, however, gave the *Queen Mary* plenty of trouble one day shortly after World War II. She arrived from Southampton as an 80-mile-an-hour gale was blowing, and her Captain decided to anchor just inside the outer breakwater and take on the America-bound passengers by tender. After a long and difficult job of loading people, baggage, and cargo, the *Mary*'s Master found one of his anchors fouled by an old German submarine cable placed in the harbor during the war. Before he was through with that tangle, the persistent gale blew the big *Queen* Ship aground and damaged her plates. Tugs pulled her off, and with the entire Russian United Nations delegation aboard, the *Mary* steamed slowly back to Southampton for repairs. It took four days to patch her up with 100 tons of concrete, before she could leave for New York.

On the *Elizabeth*'s Voyage 424, the Cherbourg pilot, Captain Burel, took over at noon, April 18, just as the ship's clocks were advanced an hour for the sixth time—to catch up with European Summer Time. According to the log, therefore, it was shortly after 1 p.m. when the *Queen Elizabeth* steamed slowly through the Passe de l'Ouest, the breakwater's western passage. The opening was more than wide enough to accept the liner, but a downward view from the wings of her bridge gave the impression that the immense ship was in a tight squeeze. From the port wing, you could look directly down upon the large, stone Fort de l'Ouest, overlooking the breakwater's western end. As the liner slowly completed her passage through the Passe de l'Ouest and into the Grande Rade, Captain Burel called out: "Steer one-two-four." The command was repeated around the wheelhouse in contrasting British accents, and Chief Quartermaster Bell brought the liner slightly to port, setting a course directly toward an opening in the harbor's inner breakwater, leading to the Petite Rade.

Behind the bridge on the *Elizabeth*'s open decks, passengers crowded the rails to see the harbor. As the ship steamed through the Passe de l'Ouest they had their first good look at the man-made outer breakwater whose construction was started in the reign of Louis XV and completed in that of Napoleon III. The breakwater is really a long, narrow island built in ten fathoms of water to protect the U-shaped harbor. The French navy first sank ninety huge foundation cones of timber packed with stones and mortar, only to have them demolished by storms and waves. But they tenaciously continued dumping material into the water until the island began to form. Eventually the sea helped, piling rubble on the artificial structure. In time the builders had a base solid enough for an impregnable breakwater with three forts, one at each end and one in the middle. It was completed in 1853 at a tremendous cost, not only in money but in lives. In one storm alone some four hundred men were trapped and killed on the unfinished breakwater.

After the *Elizabeth* was past the outer breakwater, she was joined by four tugboats, which in a few minutes were made fast to the liner. The Cherbourg tugboats, owned by the Société Cherbourgeoise de Remorquage and Sauvetage, can't compare with Moran's powerful tugs in New York, yet they are capable of handling the port's largest vessels, the two *Queen* Ships, except in heavy winds. The French tugs have no radio communication, so their masters working on a liner's bow are instructed by the pilot who blows a high pitched mouth whistle as he stands on the flying bridge. The stern tugs are instructed by toots from the liner's horns.

As the *Queen Elizabeth* entered the Petit Rade and moved slowly up to the quay, two of the four tugs pressed her port bow to hold her stem against the wind pushing on the starboard bow. As the ship glided slowly by the outer end of the quay, and her bow came into the lee of the terminal building, it tended to swing to starboard, while her stern wanted to come to port. But two tugs on the port quarter pushed hard to hold the *Elizabeth* parallel to the quay. As Captain Burel signaled his two stern tugs with the liner's horns, the booming bass echoes bounced from the nearby bluffs of Cherbourg's Montagne du Roule, famous as the main German resistance point following the 1944 Allied invasion. Between the blasts of the ship's horns, the pilot blew his shrill little mouth whistle to get action from his bow tugs. And all the time he politely called out orders for telegraph settings which put the *Elizabeth*'s propellers to work helping the maneuver.

Captain Burel first had to keep the liner from being

swung around by the uneven force of the wind. Second, he had to take the vessel slowly forward to bring her in line with the terminal's gangways. And finally he had to move the *Queen* sidewise toward the quay. Had his tugs been more powerful, the job would have been easier, but they were not that strong, and every ounce of their forward thrust had to be applied judiciously.

As time went on, Commodore Marr grew somewhat tense. He stood beside the pilot on the starboard wing and concerned himself with every inch of the liner's sidewise progress toward her proper position along the quay, which was still a good 100 feet off the starboard beam. The two men were so involved with the ship's problems that they paid no attention to the large crowd of passengers on the open decks a few yards below, and to the rear of the flying bridge. Many were watching the ship's master and the French pilot, but most were waving at a large group of people who were in the distant terminal waiting for their friends to disembark.

As more and more of the *Elizabeth*'s hull slipped into the lee of the terminal building, one bow tug was ordered aft to help those holding the stern against the wind. About that time two small motorboats rushed out from the quay, fore and aft of the liner. Each caught some small lines dropped from the steamship and dragged them back to where they could be hauled in by groups of workers waiting on the quay. The men, as in tug-of-war, pulled the lines which, in turn, towed in the large, heavy head and stern ropes, and a forward and after backspring. When these were secured to the quay, the ship's capstans were used to apply tension upon the ropes, and the liner was slowly dragged to her final stopping place. When she was made fast, and the first gangway was in place, it was exactly 2 p.m. local time.

The majority of passengers on Voyage 424 disembarked at Cherbourg and boarded a special train for Paris. During

the half hour it required for them to leave the ship, dockworkers and crane operators worked quickly to remove baggage, mail, and cargo from the *Elizabeth*'s hold. They finished
shortly after 3 o'clock, and the liner was made ready for
the undocking. Her officers and crew quickly returned to their
stations, gangways were landed, and Commodore Marr ordered his ship released. Captain Burel, who had remained on
the bridge, gave the verbal commands, and blew the liner's
horns and his mouth whistle to move the *Queen* out of Cherbourg.

His tugs pulled the long liner's stern out into the Petite
Rade, while the ship's engines backed her slowly away from
the quay. The wind, formerly a hazard, was now used to help
swing the stern to port. The bow tugs down on the port side
then shoved the stem around to the north, along the length of
the quay, until it left the lee of the terminal building. As the
liner began to turn, the westerly wind caught the port bow
and helped her around. The tugs, the ship's propellers, and
the wind together revolved the massive *Elizabeth* in a clockwise direction until she stood on a course toward the opening
in the inner breakwater. Then she steamed slowly off on her
own, and in a few minutes the French tugs left.

As she moved out across the double harbor, Captain
Burel talked with Commodore Marr about Cherbourg's problems as a port. The pilot is one of many in the city who are
trying to rebuild the business of the ancient seaport. Cherbourg was once the site of the Roman station of Coriallum,
and before that, in the Bronze Age, was the point of departure
for traders leaving for the British Isles. Some of Cherbourg's
poorer business days have come since World War II. While
the British *Queen* Ships have continued using Cherbourg because of its especially fine, deep channels, most trans-Atlantic
ships pass by in favor of Le Havre. Men like Captain Burel
intend to change the imbalance by making Cherbourg a much

more competitive port. Evidence of this effort was visible from
the *Elizabeth*'s bridge. Construction could be seen to the west,
designed to improve the port by providing better facilities for
modern ships.

At 4:30 the liner was back in the English Channel and
the winter pilot boat had come for Captain Burel. He shook
hands with Commodore Marr, who said, "See you in Southampton Thursday."

"Yes, sir," said the pilot, and he walked out of the wheelhouse, waving and bidding everyone good-bye. On Thursday
he would take a ferryboat across the English Channel to
Southampton where he would board the *Elizabeth,* as she
began Voyage 425. By so doing, he would save the ship time
and operating expenses, for she could come straight into
Cherbourg without slowing down to pick up the pilot. Reducing and increasing the speed of the world's largest liner is
costly enough to make Captain Burel's trip to Southampton
worthwhile.

Indeed, as the *Elizabeth* left Cherbourg a pilot from
Southampton was supposed to be aboard but wasn't. He had
intended to fly to the French city from the Isle of Wight, but
the plane had been delayed by bad weather. A launch would
now bring him out to the ship near the Isle of Wight that
evening.

"One four four revolutions," ordered the Commodore as
the *Queen Elizabeth* headed across the English Channel for
home. In 64 miles she would pick up her next pilot.

Meanwhile most of the passengers who had left the ship
at Cherbourg were on a fast train for Paris some 230 miles and
three and a half hours away.

Chapter XXI

The End of Voyage 424

The late afternoon was warm and beautiful as the *Queen Elizabeth* steamed across the English Channel on a course almost directly north toward the Isle of Wight and Southampton. The sun was shining upon the liner's port side, and her exterior decks were pleasant places to be. Several of the remaining passengers sat on the new lido deck on the ship's stern and sunned themselves.

On the navigation bridge, however, the officers and men

were not at all relaxed, for they were in some of the busiest waters of the entire voyage. Furthermore, in crossing the Channel, the liner was steaming at right angles to the busy traffic lanes running through the comparatively narrow water-way between England and France. The watch officers and crew had to remain especially alert.

Shortly after 6 p.m., Commodore Marr ordered propeller revolutions reduced to 115, and then roughly every half hour he called for further reductions, until they were down to 60, and the ship was making only ten knots. The Commodore was in no hurry now, for his landing at Southampton was dependent on tidal conditions that would not occur until late that evening.

At 7:30 p.m. the *Elizabeth* was just southeast of the Isle of Wight, now visible off the liner's port beam. Ahead in the sea a light appeared, and as the liner proceeded, one could see the light was mounted on a dark object projecting from the sea. "Nab Tower!" called out the officer who first saw the light. The Nab Tower marks the beginning of a 24-mile curling channel leading up around the eastern side of the Isle of Wight and eventually to Southampton. Since World War I, the tower has been well known to navigators. It was originally one of three submarine listening devices developed, but never used, in World War I. After the war, it was towed out to replace a lightship at a point in the Channel east of the Isle of Wight. It was submerged, with only the top part of the tower projecting from the water. It was equipped with a light and rooms for three lighthouse keepers. Today the tower has a fog horn and bell, radar and radio aids to navigation.

As the *Queen Elizabeth* steamed slowly around the Nab Tower into the channel, she was approached by a motor launch, which came out of the gray twilight from off the Isle of Wight. The little boat swung around the *Elizabeth*'s stern and came into her starboard side where a shell door had been opened.

"Dead slow ahead!" commanded Commodore Marr as the launch appeared. The ship's telegraphs were adjusted with the usual ringing of bells, and she slowed to seven knots so two pilots could board from the launch.

In about ten minutes the pilots arrived in the wheelhouse and one of them greeted Commodore Marr with two questions that are traditional with English pilots. "Are you well, sir? Is there any sickness aboard?"

"All is well," said the Commodore, as he greeted the arrivals with a quick salute.

The pilots were Captains Bruce Bell and Allen Smith, two of some seven hundred licensed by the venerable Corporation of Trinity House of London, which dates back to May 20, 1514, when King Henry VIII granted the organization's first Charter of Incorporation. The Trinity House Charter, changed many times from its original form, now spells out three principal missions for the corporation: the compulsory pilotage of foreign ships; the exclusive right of Trinity House to license pilots; the making of rules, regulations and by-laws for navigation.

Captains Bell and Smith, as with their counterparts in the New York's Sandy Hook Association, are self-employed, and fees are paid directly to them. The pilots in turn pay Trinity House a fee of sixpence on every pound they earn. A pilot's position with Trinity House is one of England's most coveted maritime jobs, and there are few openings. When a man is accepted, his training is long and arduous as he rises through three classes of pilots on the way to the top. In the third and lowest class he pilots vessels measuring no more than 4,500 tons; in second class, no more than 20,000 tons; and in first class he is bound by no restrictions on vessel size. Captains

Bell and Smith were, of course, first-class pilots. Moreover, they are among a very few pilots selected by Cunard to handle the *Queen* Ships, a choice which Trinity House allows shipping companies when possible.

Captain Smith took over the pilotage job soon after entering the wheelhouse, and Captain Bell remained at one side chatting with Commodore Marr. Captain Smith is an "inbound pilot," who takes a vessel from the vicinity of the Nab Tower up the channel to a point near Southampton's docks. Captain Bell, higher in seniority, is an "outbound pilot," whose work includes docking, undocking, and piloting ships out to sea. Ordinarily the *Queen* Ships' outbound pilot is Captain Jack Holt, but at the time of Voyage 424 he was on vacation. Captain Bell, the "second" Cunard pilot for the *Queens,* was replacing Captain Holt.

As Captain Smith called out the various headings, engine settings and speeds to take the *Elizabeth* up and around the Isle of Wight, it grew dark, and the sea around the slow-moving liner picked up a thousand reflections from lights on the surrounding shores and nearby vessels. It was a lovely warm evening, so Commodore Marr frequently stood on either wing of his bridge to watch the ship's progress. On the starboard beam the night sky was aglow with the lights of Portsmouth to the north. From the port side he could see smaller patches of light from a number of towns along the Isle of Wight. Cowes Road, famous for international yacht racing, was off the port bow.

A few minutes before 9 p.m. Commodore Marr stood beside Captain Smith in the wheelhouse intently watching the channel ahead, for the *Elizabeth* was approaching the buoys which mark the channel around the Bramble Bank, the most difficult stretch of water from the Nab Tower to Southampton. The vast submerged bank is found to the right of the point where the channel from the tower merges with the

Solent, another channel that leads out to the sea along the northwestern side of the Isle of Wight. A vessel coming up from the tower must make a comparatively sharp U-turn to starboard to go around "the Brambles." Taking the *Queen Elizabeth* around the turn is a task only for the most masterful navigators—as the liner's history reveals.

Shortly after her maiden voyage in 1946, she was entering Southampton one night at the end of one of her rougher crossings from New York, and the officers and crew were glad to be near home in sheltered waters. But as they steamed around the Brambles, at only three or four knots, the turn to starboard was misjudged, and the huge liner slowly buried her stem in the underwater bank. She dragged to a stop so gently that her captain didn't know she had gone aground until the ship stopped. It was all so gentle that the captain and pilot expected to back right off the bank, but the *Elizabeth* couldn't be budged even with all four engines full astern. Tugs were quickly called to assist the ship, but they couldn't move her. Some 1,065 tons of fuel and 2,610 tons of water were pumped overboard to lighten the liner, but this didn't help. As the hours went by, the chances of getting the *Elizabeth* off the Brambles diminished for the tide was receding, and the liner was settling even more solidly into the muck. A concerted effort of tugs and the liner's engines failed to pull her off during the next morning's high tide, and it was then decided to remove the passengers by tender. Many of them were unhappy about the delay, and several complained of not being promptly informed of what was happening to the vessel. That evening large crowds lined the shores to view the world's largest liner stuck in the mud, a fact that was making headlines all over the world. As the flood tide lifted the ship, sixteen tugs aided the liner's engines in the struggle to pull her astern. After a half hour the tugs and the ship's propellers finally gave a coordinated pull that succeeded. The great steamship slid slowly backward and disappeared into a bank of fog approaching from the Solent.

Because of the fog the *Queen Elizabeth* had to wait until morning to dock at Southampton, fifty hours late. At a news conference her Captain, C. M. Ford, explained the grounding. "It was a technical matter," he said. "The ship was swinging. I would say that with deep-drafted ships when they are swinging round, they are liable to 'smell' [feel] the bottom which detracts from the swing.

"In calculating the swing in the channel you have to keep headway on the ship so as to make your turn, but on this occasion the ship did not respond, even with the action of the propellers to assist. It was not a mechanical fault. No ship runs on lines. Turning a ship in a channel is purely a matter of judgment, and ever since Adam it has been human to err, whoever he is. In deep water the *Queen Elizabeth* would have responded without any trouble, but with the water so shallow —it was a neap tide—she seemed sluggish."

For two days after she finally landed, divers surveyed the liner's bottom for damage and found nothing serious. But the event forever notified masters and pilots that a trip with the *Queen Elizabeth* around the Brambles is always to be taken with great care.

On Voyage 424, the Commodore and the pilot became even more concerned than usual, for across the Brambles they could see another vessel, a tanker, proceeding down the channel they would soon be using in making the difficult turn. They certainly didn't want to meet this other ship right in the sharp curve which has absolutely no room for a second vessel when one is the *Queen Elizabeth*. The Trinity House pilot, Captain Smith, picked up a radio telephone installed in the wheelhouse for his use and talked to a traffic controller in ancient Calshot Castle, located on a point north of the Brambles. The controller, who keeps tabs by radar on all the traffic coming and going from Southampton, agreed to warn the tanker captain to avoid a meeting with the *Elizabeth* by the Brambles. However, the controller said his radar picture indicated there would be no problem, even as the vessels were now proceeding.

It was soon time to begin the turn, and Captain Smith called out the commands for changing the *Elizabeth*'s course with her wheel and her engines. Slowly the liner came around to starboard while everyone watched the oncoming tanker. For a moment it appeared that the tanker captain was turning to port and would therefore pass the liner on the inside of the curve she was making. This would break the usual rule of the road which says that ships shall pass port to port, but under the circumstances, starboard to starboard might be judged a better maneuver. But the tanker then stayed her course in the channel, though her captain was obviously moving with extreme caution. And just as well, for in the end, the concern about the meeting was unnecessary; they passed after the *Elizabeth* had come around the Brambles.

A short distance more and Captain Smith ordered the big liner to port on a second sharp turn in the channel around Calshot Castle. When she came out of this curve, the *Elizabeth* had completed a backward "S" starting from below the Bramble Bank. Now she was on a long, fairly straight run through "Southampton Water" all the way to the Ocean Dock and her passenger terminal. The liner proceeded at "Half Ahead" and "Slow Ahead," because Southampton Water, like New York, has a depth limit that barely accommodates the *Queen* Ships. But of all the ships through the centuries that have plied Southampton Water few have hurried. This course, now lined with oil refineries and other big industrial installations, once carried the galleys of the Emperor Claudius who arrived with his legions in A.D. 43 to establish the military station Clausentum. Centuries later, Southampton had become the

shipping center for English wool, and her long channel saw
Venetian merchants in their galleys and Genoese in their
beautiful carracks. And several hundred years after that
Southampton Water carried the *Mayflower* and the *Speed-
well,* leaving with the Pilgrims from the Old World to the
New.

As her 424th voyage was ending, the *Queen Elizabeth*
steamed slowly up to Southampton through the lovely April
night. She was riding the flood tide about two hours before
high water slack. This timing provided ample depth for the
giant liner, and allowed her to use the tidal flow for added
power to help swing her stern around to port so she would be
in line with the dockside.

Opposite Netley, a town below Southampton, the outbound pilot, Captain Bell, took over from the inbound pilot,
Captain Smith. In a few minutes, the running lights of six
tugs could be seen coming toward the *Elizabeth* from the
brightly lit city ahead. They swarmed around the ship, two on
the starboard bow, two on the port quarter, and two amidships on the port side. Deck hands began heaving lines, and the
huge liner was soon made fast to the six tugs.

Captain Bell communicated with the *Elizabeth*'s brood of
tugboats by radio as they slowly steamed together toward the
Ocean Dock with its large Ocean Terminal, now on the starboard bow. The tugs of Southampton are operated by two
firms, the Isle of Wight Towing Company and the Alexandra
Towing Company, both of which were represented by the
tugs distributed around the *Queen* Ship.

Captain Bell, who has a crisp, fairly high-pitched voice
with the most refined of English accents, began giving the
commands that would bring the *Elizabeth* around into the
Ocean Dock. The dock was now opposite the knighthead on
the starboard side and at right angles to the ship. The Trinity
House pilot, with absolutely no trace of excitement in his

voice, might have been asking someone to pass a plate at a dinner table as he commanded the liner's quartermasters and the tug masters who received his orders by radio down on the darkened side of the big ship.

"Half ahead two port!" he said in his polite tones at one point. "Full astern two starboard."

The commands were repeated by the officers and men on the bridge and the telegraphs were adjusted. As the order was executed, the two starboard propellers pulled hard to the rear, while the port engines pushed forward, and together they helped turn the ship clockwise upon her center.

Addressing the tugboat captains, the Trinity House pilot got them to apply tremendous outside force to the *Elizabeth* for the turning effort. Two tugs on the starboard bow moved away from the liner until their large lines were taut. Then they slowly began to pull as hard as they could. The two tugboats on the port quarter headed off in the opposite direction until their lines were pulling the liner's stern out into the channel away from the docks. On the port beam the last two tugs placed their padded bows against the riveted black hull amidships and applied power. They acted as the pivot on which the liner turned about her center. In addition to the power of the ship's engines and the other tugboats, the center two also countered the force of the tide which was beginning to help sweep the *Elizabeth*'s stern around. With all six tugs churning water, their engines' roar echoed across the railroad yards and down the dark streets lined with commercial buildings near the Southampton water front. The *Queen* slowly revolved until the full force of the tide struck the starboard quarter, and then no man-made power was needed to move the liner's after end up the channel.

Just as the revolving ship was parallel with her dock, Captain Bell ordered a change in telegraph settings, and the engines were adjusted so all the propellers pushed forward on the vessel. The two tugs amidships remained in a position to hold the liner against the tide, but the other four tugs swerved around so as to pull her forward.

Ten minutes later the first line was ashore, and soon all of her ropes were out and made fast to the pier. She was then slowly hauled into the correct position to accept gangways from the Ocean Terminal. At 10:30 that evening she was completely secured in her traditional home port, though her port of registry is Liverpool, the English city that for decades was the home of the Cunard Line.

Many of the passengers disembarked that night and left for their final destinations. Those who cared to remain aboard for the night were allowed to disembark the next morning. Most of those who remained overnight were taking a train to London, and they didn't care to make the two-hour trip so late that night.

As the liner's engines were stopped and she was made fast, Commodore Marr bid the pilots good night and went below to his quarters. In a few minutes he left the ship with his luggage, walked through the large modern passenger terminal, and took an escalator down to the street level. There he was met by a car and driven to his home at a village in the New Forest near Southampton. He came back to the ship briefly during the next two days, but most of the time he rested or worked in his garden where things were just beginning to bloom.

Many members of the *Queen Elizabeth*'s large crew who could be spared for a few hours before the beginning of Voyage 425 rushed home to see their families, but at best the visits were hurried. Of course, some crew members had time off, and they went home for a couple of weeks while the *Elizabeth* would make a round-trip voyage to New York. Their places would be filled by others returning from time off.

The liner, meanwhile, had to be prepared to leave for

New York again on Thursday morning. She was thoroughly cleaned and restocked in every way. Oil was again pumped into her tanks. Wave after wave of trucks arrived with stores, from ice cream to shoe polish. Deliveries came around the clock on carefully arranged schedules designed to prevent traffic jams. Inspections and repairs were carried out in the engine room, especially on equipment that could be looked over only when the ship was not running. All day Tuesday and Wednesday two men in boatswain seats hung over the sides of the mammoth ship, painting her hull where required. Meanwhile the liner's kitchens continued feeding crew members and a couple of hundred special visitors who came aboard for various reasons.

Then came Thursday morning. The Commodore was back, and he walked briskly up the first-class gangway. "Good morning," he said to his officers and crew as he met them enroute to his quarters. "I hope we do better this crossing. Spring is certainly here in England. I hope it's that way from here to New York."

At midday she had her passengers from England, and with the outbound Trinity House pilot, Captain Jack Holt, the *Queen Elizabeth* began Voyage 425. As she set off down Southampton Water, a small sightseeing boat filled with school children rushed out from the shore. The boat swung into the big ship's starboard side, dropped back to the stern, and then came around to the port beam. The youngsters were amazed by the gigantic liner. "There's nothing like her," said the man conducting the sightseeing tour. "There never has been. There never will be."

He was right, except in legend, where the *Merry Dun of Dover* comes closest to being matched in real life by the *Queen* Ships. The *Merry Dun of Dover* had masts so tall they had to be hinged to get under the moon and sun. Her captain once ordered his cabin boys to the top of the masts; when they returned, they were bearded old men. Navigation was no problem because a man in the crow's-nest could see all the shores of any ocean. Once she nearly got stuck in the English Channel because her beam was so wide, but the captain had her starboard side lathered with soap, and she slipped through —which accounts for the white cliffs of Dover. Another time as she tried to turn around in the Channel, her headbooms swung over Dover and scraped an entire regiment of soldiers into the sea. Commands on the *Merry Dun of Dover* were given through monstrous conch shells that could be heard a hundred miles. To inspect the entire ship the captain had to take a three-week trip on horseback. Like the *Queen* Ships, she was fast. When the *Merry Dun of Dover* made a round-trip crossing on the Atlantic she was always able to follow her own wake home. And the *Merry Dun of Dover* was a lovely vessel on which to travel, for she was lined with luxurious inns every few hundred feet apart from stem to stern. The legend does not say what happened to the *Merry Dun of Dover*, but undoubtedly she experienced a fate similar to that befalling the *Queen* Ships. Time left her in its wake.

Soon after Voyage 424 the *Queen Elizabeth* would cross the Atlantic for the last time. Being the biggest liner ever built was not enough to keep her on the seas indefinitely. Sir Basil Smallpeice, the Cunard Chairman who had to retire the *Queen* Ships, explained: "We do not intend to operate passenger ships just because they exist, if in fact they are not capable of making profits in today's and, more especially, tomorrow's markets." Faced with the insurmountable problems of the real world, the *Elizabeth* would soon follow her sister ship, the *Mary*, into retirement. Regardless of what this fate meant to their immense tonnage, the *Queen* Ships had already earned a firm place in legend.

APPENDICES

APPENDIX A

Statistical Comparison Among Cunard Superliners Built by John Brown and Company Ltd., Clydebank, Scotland

	Queen Elizabeth	Queen Mary	Queen Elizabeth 2 (facts available 1967)
GROSS TONNAGE:	82,997	81,237	58,000 approx.
LENGTH (OVERALL)	1,031 feet	1,019 ft. 6 ins.	963 feet
BEAM:	118 feet	118 feet	105 feet
KEEL TO BASE OF FUNNEL:	131 feet	125 feet	134 feet
HEIGHT OF FUNNEL:	56 feet	59 feet	67 ft. 3 ins.
OVERALL HEIGHT OF SHIP TO TOP OF FUNNEL:	187 feet	184 feet	201 ft. 3 ins.
HEIGHT TO TOP OF MAST:	233 feet	236 feet	202 ft. 3 ins.
DRAUGHT:	39 ft. $6\frac{1}{2}$ ins.	39 ft. $4\frac{1}{2}$ ins.	32 ft. 6 ins.
SERVICE SPEED:	$28\frac{1}{2}$ knots	$28\frac{1}{2}$ knots	$28\frac{1}{2}$ knots
PASSENGER CAPACITY:	2,082	1,948	2,025
MACHINERY:	Single reduction geared turbines	Single reduction geared turbines	Double reduction geared turbines
POWER:	160,000 shaft hp	160,000 shaft hp	110,000 shaft hp
NO. OF PROPELLERS:	4	4	2
NO. OF BOILERS:	12	24	3

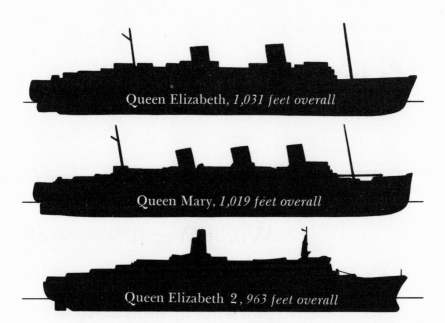

Queen Elizabeth, *1,031 feet overall*

Queen Mary, *1,019 feet overall*

Queen Elizabeth 2, *963 feet overall*

	Queen Elizabeth	*Queen Mary*	*Queen Elizabeth 2*
NO. OF DECKS:	13	12	13
SWIMMING POOLS:	2 indoor, 1 outdoor	2 indoor	2 outdoor, 2 indoor
OFFICERS AND CREW:	1,280	1,260	1,000 (approx.)
CARGO SPACE:	46,295	44,690½	—
DATE OF BUILDING CONTRACT:	Oct. 6, 1936	Dec. 1, 1930	Dec. 30, 1964
LAUNCHED:	Sept. 27, 1938	Sept. 26, 1934	Sept. 20, 1967
NAMING CEREMONY BY:	Her Majesty Queen Elizabeth	Her Majesty Queen Mary	Her Majesty Queen Elizabeth II
MAIDEN VOYAGE		May 27, 1936	—
SECRET WARTIME	March 2, 1940 Clyde-N.Y.	Southampton-N.Y.	
COMMERCIAL	Oct. 16, 1946 Southampton-N.Y.		
RETIRED	1968 Philadelphia, Pa.	1967 Long Beach, California	—

APPENDIX B

World War II Service of *Queen* Ships Carrying U.S. Troops to Australia and United Kingdom

Reported by U.S. War Department, March 15, 1946

	Number of Passengers	Cost
Queen Elizabeth	465,904	$46,896,025
Queen Mary	436,707	$43,981,725
Total:	902,611	$90,877,750

APPENDIX C

Additional Facts About the
World's Largest Liner, the
Queen Elizabeth

STRUCTURAL AND OPERATIONAL

PROPELLERS
4. Each weighs 32 tons and is 18 feet in diameter.

RUDDER
140 tons. Streamlined with hull. Door in the side allows internal inspection.

ANCHORS
3. Each weighs about 16 tons and has 990 feet of chain cable with links 2 feet long. The three cables weigh 225 tons.

LIFEBOATS
26. Each has 145-person capacity and is driven by a high-speed diesel engine.

NAME LETTERS ON BOWS

2½ feet high. Occupy some 68 feet.

HULL

Built of riveted steel plates, 8 to 30 feet long. Has double bottom with intervening space of nearly six feet. Has double shell around machinery spaces up to 40 feet on hull.

RIVETS

10,000,000.

METAL

50,000 tons in hull and machinery.

PORTHOLES AND WINDOWS

2,000.

WATERTIGHT COMPARTMENTS

140. Combination of longitudinal subdivisions of ship and 15 watertight bulkheads dividing ship transversely.

MAIN ENGINES

4 sets of single reduction geared turbines with total of 257,000 blades.

HORSEPOWER

160,000 shaft horsepower, total of 4 shafts.

BOILERS

12 water tube boilers supply steam with pressure of 425 lbs. per sq. inch at 750 degrees F.

ELECTRIC POWER

2 separate power stations, total 8,800 kw., sufficient to supply small city.

BRIDGE

125 feet wide, wing to wing, 90 feet above water.

STEERING WHEELS

2. One auxiliary in case main wheel fails.

COMPASSES

2. Gyro compasses indicate true geographical North. Control

several smaller gyro compasses (repeaters) located on bridge and in other parts of ship. Main gyro compasses guide automatic steering gear equipment, known as "Metal Mike" or "The Iron Man." Ship also contains magnetic compasses as auxiliaries.

WHISTLES

3. Each weighs one ton, can be heard 10 miles at sea. Blown from any of five controls on bridge.

RADIO

4 main transmitters cover short-, medium-, and long-wave. Complete radiotelegraph and radiotelephone service.

TELEPHONES

680. Used within the ship, to connect with municipal systems in port, and to radiotelephone all over the world when at sea.

HOSPITAL

Includes general hospitals (passenger and crew), isolation hospital, operating theater, dispensary, and medical inspection room, including complete dental chair, X-ray equipment, and short-wave diathermy equipment.

KITCHENS

5. One combined for first and cabin classes, one for tourist class, one for Verandah Grill, one kosher, and one crew. Staffed by about 125 ratings.

EARTHENWARE, CHINA, AND GLASS

100,000 pieces.

SILVERWARE

26,000 pieces.

LINEN

210,000 towels, 30,000 sheets, 31,000 pillow cases, 21,000 table-cloths.

APPENDIX D

Description of the
Queen Elizabeth's
Outstanding Public Rooms

The following is reprinted in part from a Cunard fact sheet on the *Queen Elizabeth* prepared soon after World War II. It presents a picture of the ship's most impressive public rooms close to what they were like when the liner was first used commercially. Some of the rooms were changed during the 1950's and 1960's, but not substantially.

First Class

THE FIRST-CLASS RESTAURANT
This is approached on "R" deck through a high foyer, containing a large coat of arms of Her Majesty Queen Elizabeth, carved in lime-tree wood by Bainbridge Copnall, the carving being sup-

ported on the port and starboard sides by a carved Elizabethan herald by the same artist.

Inside the Restaurant, above the entrance, is a silken replica of the Queen's personal standard, which commemorates Her Majesty's visit to the liner on October 8, 1946, when, together with Their Royal Highnesses, Princess Elizabeth and Princess Margaret, Her Majesty was aboard the *Queen Elizabeth* during trials.

The center portion of the Main Restaurant is higher than the outboard areas which are divided into three large bays on either side and have daylight lighting with a view of the sea. The center portion has a canopy at ceiling level which is richly decorated with gilded ornament. The four piers are sheathed with ornamental metalwork, framed with colored leather, bronze, and woodwork.

A large clock face, placed centrally both port and starboard, has been carved in lime-tree wood by Bainbridge Copnall, taking the form of signs of the Zodiac round the clock face itself. The same sculptor carved a series of wood panels finished with silver leaf round the entrances, and two large vigorous groups at the after end of the Restaurant, one representing "The Fisherman" and the other "The Huntress."

Between these two groups hangs a large tapestry specially designed by two South African artists, Eleanor Esmonde-White and Leroux Smith Leroux.

PRIVATE DINING ROOMS

Adjoining the Main Restaurant are three private dining rooms— two on the starboard side, one on the port side. The forward starboard dining room has been paneled in a rare and striking veneer of oyster aspen. A large decorative glass panel, designed by Jan Juta, occupies a lighted recess on the inboard side. The after private dining room on the starboard side is paneled in English elm burr. The after port dining room is treated with claret-and-white leather. An illuminated recess contains a large decorative metal panel executed by means of metal spray guns, and designed by Jan Juta.

There is a small intimate Cocktail Bar on the port side beside the entrance to the Restaurant foyer, paneled in champagne-colored leather, bleached white London plane tree and sycamore curl and containing another decorative panel by Jan Juta.

THE MAIN STAIRS

The walls of the stairs are lined with Arbele, which is an English poplar burr. The staircase balustrades are of silver-bronze, and the head portions are covered with leather. The various halls at deck level are paneled with English olive ash burr and myrtle burr. At "B" deck level one is able to look through windows into the Restaurant. The Main Hall on the Main Deck contains a large shop, and one eventually reaches the Main Hall Promenade Deck. In this Hall, at the head of the stairs is a rich sculptural group by Maurice Lambert, A.R.A. He has also executed a group, port and starboard, for the doors to the Promenade Deck, and two other figures, each in a niche on either side of the doorway to the Main Lounge. On the forward wall, opposite the entrance to the Main Lounge, is a large marquetry panel, "Canterbury Pilgrims," designed by George Ramon and executed by J. Dunn. The walls of this Main Hall (Promenade Deck) are covered in two tones of cream leather. In the Main Hall itself are located the radio, travel, shops and telephone services. Leading off it forward on the starboard side is the Library with a raised gallery and bookcases on either side.

OBSERVATION LOUNGE AND COCKTAIL BAR

Forward of the Main Lounge is a large Cocktail Lounge, somewhat semi-circular in plan. The whole of the outer walls of this space have been paneled in sycamore dyed to the color of lobster shell. Inlaid into this paneling are various amusing scenes from the circus, designed by George Ramon, and executed in many different kinds of wood. The inner portion of the Cocktail Lounge is paneled in silver sycamore, the woodwork being relieved with inlaid metal stars. The Lounge is designed in terraces, and the portion of the floor containing the large semi-circular bar is sunk below the rest of the room. [The lounge was originally used by first-class passengers, but later it was open only to tourist class.]

THE MAIN LOUNGE

The impressive entrance to the Lounge is at the after end of the Main Hall. Canadian maple cluster with a finishing of elm burr of a delicate tawny pink are the predominating woods in the room. The veneer is relieved by a quantity of leather-covered paneling in light gray, pale blue, and buff. The central portion of the Lounge rises to a height of some 23 feet. Most arresting feature is Sir Oswald Birley's painting of Her Majesty Queen Elizabeth, which occupies a prominent position at the end of the room immediately facing the entrance.

Small marquetry panels, their design based on old playing cards, by George Ramon, and framed with decorative leather and wood carving contribute to the tasteful colorings of the room. Two flower study paintings by Cedric Morris occupy a central position at the forward end of the outboard portions. Writing recesses are provided in various parts of the room.

THE WRITING ROOM

Leading aft from the Lounge on the port side is the Writing Room. This is an open room with the amidship stairs in the center of it, and is paneled in light-gray sycamore with decorative leather recesses for writing tables.

THE SALON

The next space aft is a large ballroom known as the Salon. The walls of this room have been covered with quilted satin and it contains several decorative features. Centrally placed on the forward bulkhead is a deep recess lined out with decorative glass hand-painted and designed by Jan Juta. On the after bulkhead is a large orchestra platform and recess equipped for colored lighting effects. Four recesses on the outboard side are lined with ivory-colored sycamore and decorated with small silver stars. The central portion of the ceiling is lined with gold mirror and contains elaborate equipment for colored lighting effects. (This space was converted and became the Midships Bar. It was then used for cocktails and for dancing in the late evening.)

THE SMOKE ROOM

This large room abaft the Salon is paneled from the various parts of a giant chestnut tree that grew on the Isle of Wight, and has four distinct varieties of veneer. On the after bulkhead are three large carvings by Dennis Dunlop representing Hunting, Fishing, and Shooting. On the forward bulkhead he has carved a large clock face. Below the clock face is a decorative map painted by Macdonald Gill which shows the relative moving positions of both the *Queen Elizabeth* and the *Queen Mary*. Two paintings by Norman Wilkinson, one of Elsinore and the other of Dover Harbor, occupy prominent positions in the room.

CINEMA THEATER

Further aft is the Cinema Theater, seating 338 persons. This theater can also be approached from the after end by Cabin passengers. It has a small stage for ship's concerts, etc., and the general color scheme is red, white and blue. The carpet is blue, the chair upholstery vermilion, and walls of finished ivory. Lighting is mainly by small lighthouse lenses arranged as decorative spots in the enclosing walls.

THE VERANDAH GRILL

The Verandah Grill is situated on the Sun Deck. The walls are covered in ivory-colored sycamore veneer. An illuminated decorative glass balustrade surrounds the dance floor which receives floodlighting from it. Mechanically controlled colored lighting is arranged for in the ceiling and behind the orchestra recess. A large decorated glass screen is arranged at the four corners of the central part of the room, each of which was designed by Jan Juta. Adjoining the Grill Room are completely equipped kitchens and service rooms. The main windows overlook the stern and the ship's wake in the distance.

SWIMMING POOL

Situated on "C" Deck, the Swimming Pool and surround is 51 feet long and 29 feet in width, the pool itself being 36 feet long and 16 feet wide. A latex composition filled with mother-of-pearl chippings was used on the walls of the room, and the polished surface is interlaced with wavy metal strips of silver bronze. The pool itself is finished in white briquettes, with black nosing tiles, and handrails and other fittings are of nickel alloy. The four columns at the sides of the pool are in delicately shaded sea-green mosaic, while the ceiling is stippled and painted white. Illumination is provided by a continuous trough of light, set in nickel alloy, with sandblasted glass panels, above the pool, and by a series of circular "porthole" lights inset in the surrounding walls.

Adjoining the swimming pool are Turkish and Curative baths. Walls are of light cream, with, in some rooms, low-relief tiles inset at random. Ceilings are paneled and painted white, and the floors are tiled in a margin of dark gray, with contrasting panels of light gray and coral.

DECK TENNIS AND SQUASH RACKETS COURTS AND GYMNASIUM

Extensive facilities for both deck games and promenading are provided on the Sports and Sun Decks. There is a balcony on the Sports Deck from which spectators may watch players in the Squash Rackets Court on the Sun Deck below. The Gymnasium is situated on the starboard side of the Sun Deck, near the Squash Rackets Court.

Cabin Class

MAIN STAIRCASE

The longest staircase in the ship, the Cabin Main Staircase, serves eight decks, and is provided with two passenger lifts and one baggage lift. On the Promenade Deck, the companionway opens out to the Theater, which is available to First Class or Cabin Class passengers, the Drawing Room, Library, Smoke Room, and Cocktail Bar.

The companionway at the Main Deck level opens out to the Lounge and Children's Playroom. The corridors on "B" Deck level lead to the hairdressing saloons, and at "R" Deck the companionway opens out to the Dining Saloon. At this level are situated the Purser's Office, Travel Bureau and Bank, and the radio-telephone facilities. At "E" Deck level, where the staircase begins, the Swimming Pool and Gymnasium are situated.

The treatment of the staircase flights and companionways was carried out with a dado of elm burr, edged with Australian walnut, while the frieze above was kept to a light vellum tone by bleaching Queensland silky oak. On each half landing two niches faced in black Vitroflex contain Poole pottery vases in green, which are floodlit from above. The lift casing is lined with silver sheet plastic, into which a series of abstract motifs, designed by Hector Whistler, are inlaid in aluminum foil.

LOUNGE: MAIN DECK

This is the principal social center for Cabin passengers, and is an exceptionally large air-conditioned room. The floor is covered with parquet and the loose carpets may be easily removed to provide spaces for dancing.

A feature of the after end of the room is a raised terrace, with a beautiful balustrade of silver bronze and glass, from which unusually large windows afford a view of the whole of the after part of the ship. The wall surfaces of the room are formed of cloudy vellum hide, silver bronze, and a special type of glass, manufactured from spun glass laid between sheets and silvered on the back. The general sense of airiness is enhanced by two deeply engraved maps in molded glass of the Northern and Southern Hemispheres.

The two forward bays on port and starboard sides have been arranged and equipped as small writing rooms.

CHILDREN'S PLAYROOM: MAIN DECK

This charming playroom contains two features which enchant the hearts of all children.

First, there is a small house, designed in the style of traditional fairytale illustrations, complete with colored half-timbering, inglenooks, and grotesque rafters, and with a small entrance hall, a bedroom, and a sitting room.

The other part of the room contains a miniature replica of a ship's deck and navigating bridge, complete with small-scale telegraphs, voice tube, steering wheel, and binnacle. The steering wheel on the bridge is geared to an endless panorama of sea scenes, ranging from the arctic to the tropics, which gives the illusion of movement to the children on the bridge.

SWIMMING POOL: "E" DECK

The pool is lined with golden quartzite, which, seen through the sea water, gives the impression of a sandy pool. As a foil to the gold of the pool and the cream walls of the room, the surrounds are in gray quartzite.

An experiment which proved successful was carried out on the walls, where an unbroken surface was formed in a composition of mother-of-pearl and latex. Into this plain surface are set a number of decorative motifs, designed by Hector Whistler. The ceiling over the pool is formed of panels faced and edged with cream-colored plastic, into which are laid aluminium lines.

The columns in this room are treated with lightly varied mosaic tesserae, ranging in color from deep ultramarine blue to emerald green.

A clear glass screen at the foot of the Main Staircase is fenestrated with bronze, and etched with decorative sea motifs, designed by Hector Whistler. On each side of the pool, drinking fountains in Venetian mosaic stand on low platforms of golden quartzite. All metalwork and electric light fittings are treated with the brilliant green of Pompeiian bronze. The dressing boxes have quartzite floors, partitions and walls being faced with cream plastic.

A Note About the Author

Leonard A. Stevens, a prolific free-lance writer, is the author of many books and a contributor to most of the major magazines. Born in Lisbon, New Hampshire, in 1920, he received his B.A. and M.A. degrees from the State University of Iowa. Among his recent books are *On Growing Older* (1965), written for the President's Council on Aging. He has written several juveniles, including *The Trucks That Haul by Night* (1966) and *Flight 808* (1963). Working from a long background in the science of human communication—including the books *The Ill-Spoken Word* (1966) and *Are You Listening* (1957), which he co-authored with Dr. Ralph Nichols—Mr. Stevens has completed a book on the human nervous system for publication by Alfred A. Knopf. He lives with his wife and four children in Bridgewater, Connecticut.

A Note on the Type

This book was set on the Linotype in a type face called "Baskerville." The punches for this face were cut under the supervision of George W. Jones, the eminent English printer and the designer of Granjon and Estienne. Linotype Baskerville is a facsimile cutting from type cast from the original matrices of a face designed by John Baskerville, a writing master of Birmingham, for his own private press.

John Baskerville's original face was one of the forerunners of the type-style known as "modern face" to printers: a "modern" of the period A.D. 1800.

This book was composed by The Haddon Craftsmen, Scranton, Pennsylvania, printed by Universal Lithographers, Timonium, Maryland, and bound by L. H. Jenkins, Richmond, Virginia. Designed by Anthea Lingeman.